All of us ha[...]

Most of us waste it.

As he sat in the back of the police car, hands cuffed and heading to jail, Damon was abandoning his young family like he'd been abandoned so many times as a child. Could what happened on this night finally help him overcome 30+ years of hell and heartache, or would the generational curses he so desperately wanted to stop continue through his children?

Damon grew up with alcoholism, divorce, homelessness, life in foster homes, sexual abuse, and deep rooted anger towards his parents. As an adult he struggled with bipolar, domestic violence, time in jail, depression, addiction, failed relationships, divorce, homelessness, and a teenage daughter struggling with addiction. In *Pain Drives Change* Damon shares how embracing this pain in his life transformed him. His story offers a path and practical tools for personal change in our times of pain.

PAIN
DRIVES
CHANGE

Damon Stoddard

Published by Damon Stoddard

Pain Drives Change

Copyright © 2016 by Damon Stoddard

This edition: ISBN 978-0692630020, Version 1.02

In Loving Memory of Mom

Mom,

Your courageous decisions to allow your pain to change you will break the generational dysfunction in my family. I will forever cherish the time we spent together writing this book. Our shared tears brought me closer to you than I've ever been. May all who read your letter and our story find the hope and courage to make the necessary changes in their own lives.

I love you, and I'm proud of you.

———————

Dad,

Most fathers would have given up after being treated like I treated you, but you didn't. You continued pursuing me even after I hurt you multiple times. Thank you for not giving up on me. Generations of our family will never be the same because you didn't give up on me.

I love you and respect you more today than I ever have.

———————

This book is dedicated to both of you. May my writing bring honor to each of you.

—Damon

Contents

Introduction

Finding Joy in the Trials of Life

*Consider it all joy, my brethren, when you encounter
various trials knowing that the testing of your faith produces
endurance, and let endurance have its perfect result so that you
will be perfect and complete lacking in nothing*

—James 1:2-4

The first time I read this scripture, I thought, "Seriously, how can there be joy in the trials of life?" At this point in my life, I'd certainly had my share of trials, and as best I could remember, I hadn't experienced joy in ANY of the trials.

When I was a toddler Mom and Dad decided to get a divorce, but there wasn't a lot of joy.

When, as a young child, I watched them strap Mom into a straitjacket and take her away in an ambulance, there wasn't a lot of joy.

When I woke up in the middle of the night to screams and shouts, watching my mom in a drunken rage throw plates from the china cabinet at my stepdad—I don't recall a lot of joy.

Being abandoned and living with our neighbors while Mom was in the hospital didn't bring me a lot of joy.

Living in a park in Wenatchee as a second-grader because we had been locked out of our basement apartment didn't bring much joy, either.

A family of 5 kids being torn apart and sent to different foster homes while Mom went to treatment certainly didn't bring any of us joy.

Growing up without my dad in the home didn't produce a lot of joy, either. In fact, it did exactly the opposite—it produced anger— deep-rooted anger that would later reveal itself through horrendous acts of domestic violence (DV) that I committed multiple times before finding myself in jail, a young father faced with the possibility of losing my family and my job.

I certainly didn't find any joy in these acts of abuse or my time in jail.

And I didn't find any joy on that cold, rainy night in Seattle on January 8, 1999, when I packed up my clothes and a few personal items to separate from my wife after two and a half difficult years of marriage.

I didn't feel the joy when I waved goodbye to Monica, my beautiful fifteen-month-old daughter who I swore I would never abandon like I was when I was her age.

God has a strange way of getting our attention. Five days later on January 13, 1999, I decided I was going to respond to the pain of separation in a different way than I ever had. I put a video camera on a tripod and started recording a video journal. With tears streaming down my face, I promised myself that I would allow this pain to change me, and 1 day I would use my experiences to the benefit of others in similar situations.

The scripture tells us to *consider* it all joy. It doesn't say we will *feel* joy in the trials. It tells us to make a decision, to consider it all joy in the midst of our pain. Joy is a verb, not a noun. Joy requires action. Up until then, my emotions dictated my decisions. I couldn't fathom a life in which my decisions would dictate my emotions.

However, I had professed to be a Christian, and I had

made a decision: I was going to consider it joy, and I was going to allow God to use the pain of separation to drive the change in me that He wanted to see. I don't recall the exact date, but right around the same time, I discovered the second portion of the scripture

...knowing the testing of your faith produces endurance and let endurance have its perfect result so that you will be perfect and complete, lacking in nothing.

Wow! The scripture spoke to me, and I realized that I could choose joy *because* I knew God would use the trials to transform me into the man He created me to be, and that through the trials I would become perfect and complete, lacking in nothing.

What did I have to lose? Rebelling against the trials of life had gotten me nowhere. In fact, rebelling against the trials only made things worse. I was thirty-two years old, sitting in a little red house in the worst part of Seattle with tears streaming down my face. I was severely depressed and all alone. My only daughter, Monica, was fifteen months old, going to sleep without her daddy at home. In two and a half years of marriage, I had committed multiple acts of DV against my wife, and as much as I tried, I couldn't stop doing it.

A little voice inside my head kept repeating the words I'd heard so many times from the people I loved and cared for the most. "You are a monster, you'll never change." And I believed it.

That voice was wrong. I'm now forty-seven and I am living proof that God uses pain to drive change. I'm not perfect but I am happily re-married. I have the family and life that I never dreamed possible. God has blessed nearly every aspect of my life. God knew the level of pain necessary to change me into who I am today. I know beyond the shadow of a doubt that I wouldn't be the man I am today without this pain. While I'd never want to go through the pain again, I am thankful for its results.

My hope in writing this book is that you, too, will discover how to find joy in the trials you are experiencing and that through my struggles and ultimate victories you will find the hope and tools to become the man or woman God has created you to be.

Questions to Consider

* Reflect on a season of your life when you were in pain.
  * How did you respond?
* How has this pain and your response shaped the person you are today?
* What is the greatest source of pain in your life today?
  * Given the promise of James 1:2-4, how will you respond to this pain?
* How can I help you?
* You can find more resources and my contact information at **www.paindriveschange.com**.

I
The Pain of Being Alone

*Some men came, bringing to him a paralyzed man, carried
by four of them. Since they could not get him to Jesus because
of the crowd, they made an opening in the roof above Jesus by
digging through it and then lowered the mat the man was lying
on. When Jesus saw their faith, he said to the paralyzed man,
"Son, your sins are forgiven."*
—Mark 2:3-5

Let me ask you some tough questions: If you had a crisis
in your life and you urgently needed help, do you have
anyone you could call and know, *beyond the shadow of a doubt,*
that they would be there for you? If you found yourself in sin
so shameful, do you have anyone that you feel safe enough
with to share the details and know that you wouldn't be
judged? If you were severely depressed and you couldn't get
out of bed, do you have friends that would drop everything
to encourage you and support you? If you found yourself
homeless, do you have people who would open their home
to you without question? Finally, the toughest question—
do you have someone in your life that you have given the
freedom to confront you at any time if they saw destructive
behavior in you?

I didn't; and according to a study by Patrick Means from
his book *"Men's Secret Wars"* seventy-five percent of the men
in church don't either!

How did this happen? Reflecting back on my entire life,
I've always felt alone. One of my most poignant memories as

a child came when I was in kindergarten. My mom struggled with alcoholism and I witnessed a number of drunken events that no child should see. On this particular event, I awoke from sleep to yelling and the shrill sound of ceramic plates being broken. As I stumbled into the living room, I noticed the dishes from our china cabinet were in pieces. In a sheer rage, Mom was pulling out plates and throwing them furiously at her husband, shouting and calling him names that no child should hear.

Paralyzed with fear, I joined in the screaming and crying. Unfortunately, I was alone—not physically alone but emotionally abandoned by those responsible for providing the foundation of safety and security for the rest of my life. My mom was too drunk to care for me, and my stepdad was trying his best to protect himself.

My older sister didn't know what to do. Then, I witnessed something that left an indelible imprint on my soul. She prayed to Jesus and said, "Jesus, please help Mom." Instantly, she stopped throwing china and passed out. The sheer terror I was witnessing turned into instant calm.

Here's the irony. My stepdaughters witnessed in me what I had witnessed in my mom that evening. On a cold and dreary evening in early October 1997, I did something that I will forever regret. I don't recall what triggered the incident, but I do remember that I was irritable and edgy all day. You could say I was "picking a fight." My wife and I began arguing, but it didn't stop at an argument. In a fit of rage, I yelled and screamed obscenities, but the situation only got worse. My wife grabbed Monica (just a month old at the time) and headed for the door to protect herself.

The fear of being abandoned by the woman I loved more than anyone in the world penetrated my soul. In an uncontrollable rage, I struck her with a closed fist and took

Monica from her. Fortunately, the police were there almost immediately. They cuffed me and hauled me to King County Jail. Once again, I was alone.

Sitting in King County Jail that night I had *nobody* in my life that I trusted enough to share where I was and what I'd done. There was only 1 phone number I could call with the quarter I was given for a phone call: my wife.

I remember the rage I felt in my heart. How could SHE call the police on me? SHE put me in this situation! SHE antagonized me! SHE had no right!

In those moments, I'm certain I experienced the same emotion that I believe Adam and Eve experienced in the garden after they committed their sin. I was naked (emotionally) and ashamed of myself. And just like Adam, I took no responsibility for my actions—I blamed my wife. The pain of being incarcerated was not sufficient to drive the changes that God needed to make in me. It would take 2 more years and significantly more pain before I would surrender and ask God for help. More on this later...

Mom knew she needed help, but by getting help, it meant that her 5 children would have to be taken care of. I don't know where my older siblings went, but I recall staying with some neighbors while Mom went to alcohol treatment. I wasn't physically alone, but as a young boy, I felt abandoned and all alone.

Unfortunately, Mom's stay in the hospital didn't resolve all of her issues, and she quickly began drinking again. Not long afterwards she found herself in a situation where she had 5 children to raise, but we were without a home. Fortunately, there was a family that had a basement in their home, and they opened it up for us all to live in. The basement didn't have a shower or a bath, but it did have a kitchen sink. Mom put up a garbage bag around the sink and rinsed us off with the spray nozzle from the sink to keep us clean. We were poor and this basement was our home for a short while.

One day when I came home from school (I was in second grade), Mom and the rest of my family were standing outside the door. I asked why, and I was told that we were locked out of our home and wouldn't have a place to live. I still don't know why this happened, but I do remember that same fear of being alone creeping in. My home and all my belongings were locked up.

We didn't know what to do, so we walked to the park. Now we were all alone without a home. Mom didn't know what to do, but my older brother, Dean, decided he was going to hitchhike to our home town of Grand Coulee and get a job to try to take care of us. My oldest brother, Danny, was in detention, so that left Mom with me and my 2 older sisters, D'Ann and Debbie, to take care of. We were together but all alone.

We stayed in the park for what I believe was a few days (I honestly don't know how long we were there.) What I do know is that the pain of being homeless with her children brought Mom to the level of pain she needed to finally get healthy. I can remember the day like it was yesterday. We all walked to the local DSHS office to meet with Mom's case worker, Meredith. This was forty years ago but I can still remember her name! Mom told her that she needed help, and she needed shelter for her kids.

I can only imagine the pain Mom must have experienced when she had to release her children into someone else's care. However, she knew that if she didn't change, it would be even more painful. In that instant, it was easier to give up her children than it was to try to keep her children without a home or a way to feed them.

Pain drives change. The pain of staying the same was

greater than the pain of change, so change was guaranteed. Mom made the courageous decision, and we all went into foster homes while she began a path that would ultimately free her from her alcohol addiction.

Unfortunately, there weren't any foster homes available at that time that would accept all 3 of us. I entered one foster home and my 2 sisters entered another. Not only was I separated from my mom, I was separated from my older sisters. I felt abandoned, and once again, I was alone. As a helpless 8-year-old boy, I lost every bit of security I'd ever known. The same sister who prayed for Jesus' help on that awful night a few years ago was no longer there to comfort me. My mom, even though she struggled with alcoholism, was a great mom and we were very close. She, too, had abandoned me (at least that's how it felt to an 8-year-old) and left me alone to live with a family that I didn't know.

Regretfully, my dad didn't intervene either, leaving me to feel abandoned by him and all alone. Nobody in my parents' extended family offered to care for us—not my grandparents, not my aunts, not my uncles. *Nobody.* I think it is a radical understatement to say that *I was abandoned and alone.*

I'd like to pause for a moment and share the fundamental principle of this book. This principle is profoundly simple. Teaching you this principle requires a small exercise on your part. Are you ready?

Please take a moment and go into your kitchen to the stove. Now turn the front burner on high and wait a moment until it is glowing orange (make sure it is good and hot before taking the next step). Now I want you to open your hand and place it on the hot burner. What? You aren't going to do this? Why not? Obviously, you aren't going to put your hand on the burner because you know it will cause you severe pain.

Now, imagine walking up to the stove, and accidentally

touching the hot burner. What happens next? Reflexively, you pull your hand away because the pain is so great. The pain of leaving your hand on the hot burner was greater than the pain of pulling your hand away, so you *automatically* removed it. You didn't leave your hand on the burner and say, "Hmm, this is hot. What should I do? Maybe I'll pull it off so that it doesn't get burned."

The motivation to move your hand was *automatic*. The pain was so great that it drove change. Simple, isn't it? *Pain drives change*. If you'd put your hand on the stove and the burner wasn't hot, you could have kept your hand on the stove. There was no pain; therefore, you didn't change by moving your hand.

This same principle of *Pain drives change* works in every area of your life. The pain doesn't have to be physical for it to work. The pain provides the motivation to change yourself in ways that you likely knew needed to change you but didn't have the motivation to do so. When the pain is so great, it is guaranteed that *something* will change. The question isn't whether change will happen. The question is: How will you choose to respond to the pain? If you respond in a positive way, you will grow, and your life will be better than it was prior to the pain. James 1:4 promises that. Furthermore, if we know that the trials of life will improve our character, it is no longer hard to find joy in the trials. Choosing joy will make the trials of life less painful, giving us the ability to endure. *Pain drives change*. My challenge to you is if you are in pain, embrace it and choose joy.

I want to honor my mother and father in the writing of this book. Up until now, I've only talked about my painful childhood memories. My Mom made the hardest decision of her life: to allow her pain to change her, she gave up her kids and stopped drinking so that we would have the healthy home and life she always dreamed we'd have. I've asked her to share a little bit about that time in her life, the courageous decision, and the ultimate outcome. I'm praying that her courage will inspire you to make the brave decision that you haven't been able to make.

Mom's Story

Giving up you kids was the hardest thing I'd ever done besides losing my son, Dean, in a car wreck. I was physically abused by my third husband. One time it was so bad that I had eighteen stitches in my head from being slammed against the trailer. The police were at our house all the time, and I was a drunk when I was with him, the only way I could stand to be around him was to drink. I felt trapped, and when I was told that the state wouldn't allow my oldest son, Danny, to come home because it wasn't safe; I knew I needed to make a change.

One afternoon I caught my husband in an affair. I had been drinking and had a bottle of vodka in the car. I was so angry that I wrecked a car trying to run into him and was taken to the hospital for observation. My pain was now so great that I needed to change. I made a decision that day to stop drinking. The next morning while my husband was at work our neighbors, grandma, and grandpa loaded our stuff up and we moved to a small basement apartment in Wenatchee.

We went to what we thought was a safe home in Wenatchee with my AA friends to live in a basement apartment with my 4 children while Danny stayed in foster care. We shared meals and a bathroom with the people that owned the house. We spent time at AA meetings–there were pool tables and cookies, it wasn't far up the street.

I remember it was spring and it was starting to warm up. We came home one day to find the door locked. What does a mother do? I had 4 children to take care of, and I didn't know what to do. I was really angry. I wanted to bust the door. These were my AA friends and I didn't know why they'd turned us away.

We must have gone to the park; it was close by. There was a little store, and we had a few dollars in food stamps. Twinkies and Ding Dongs were our diet. I left the children in the park to see if I could find help. I went to an AA counselor but he couldn't help me, but he said the welfare office could. That meant putting my children in foster care. I walked back to the park only to find Dean was gone. He had gone to Grand Coulee; he hitchhiked, and his ears got really sun burned. (Being a red head he was very sensitive to the sun.)

I walked to the welfare office with 3 children not knowing if I could get help. We were met by a small kind lady. I asked her if she could please help me. When she said foster care, my heart fell out. I need you to keep them together. I've been feeding them in the park and I want to keep them together. Meredith came back with the news. Damon would go to one home and Debra and D'Ann to another.

My children will be safe and my heart is broken. I have no choice, the children have to go to different homes.

We were allowed to pack some clothes in our big white suitcase, but there were very few clothes for all of us. Damon's new foster family picked him up and he drove away to stay with them. We went with Meredith to the round house where the older girls would stay.

A mother's heart is breaking. This was one of the hardest times of my life: leaving my children. Tears are flowing from the memories of that day in Wenatchee. My shopping cart and a white suitcase is all I had, but my children are safe except Dean who went to get help.

I needed to know he was ok so I hitch-hiked and caught a ride with some fishermen who took me to a motel in Grand Coulee where Dean was. He was with friends and was safe.

I asked my parents if I could work for them so I could make some money to get back to Wenatchee and get an apartment. I did a couple jobs and I still didn't have any clothes except the clothes I had on. Grandma gave me some money and I hitch-hiked back to Wenatchee. I went to the house to get some more clothes. I broke the windows and got into the house, but there was nothing there. The apartment was empty. I was locked out of my home; I had absolutely nothing but the clothes I had on. *Nobody* would help me. The accusations against me were all lies and I didn't understand why they were doing this to me. I was infuriated!

They saw me in their home and called the police. I went to jail and they did a strip search on me, thinking I was high on drugs. They put me back in the mental hospital so I could get help, but I didn't stay. I ran away and hitchhiked back to Wenatchee. Thinking back to this time I think I was having a manic episode because I'd stopped drinking and I wasn't doing drugs.

I was able to get a small basement apartment and I worked for Mary from AA in exchange for my rent. I remember I found a halter top in the alley so I now had 1 more outfit to wear. Mary's rags were my dish towels.

Debra came to live with me and I continued working toward my goal of getting all of my children back. I got a job at the bus station and got a bigger apartment where me, D'Ann and Debra lived. Damon was living at the boy's ranch and I got a job working for Gene who ran it. He had a small apartment on the side of the house and I moved there with Debra and D'Ann while Dean and Damon lived in the boy's ranch. With the exception of Danny, my whole family was together.

The state said I couldn't live there while working on the property, so Gene put a mobile home on the back of the property. I only lived there for a couple weeks before I packed everyone up and we all moved to Grand Coulee in a little house without any hot water. We were poor but managed to live on my Social Security check. Gene bought me a car and paid gas so that I could drive Damon back and forth to Gene's and earn some extra money during the weekends.

My 3 children were once again together as we lived in this small house. I refused to pay the rent because there wasn't any hot water and we were evicted. Debra had gotten married, but my 3 remaining children moved into the low income apartments.

I met a man and very quickly started drinking again. I knew I was going downhill but he promised he'd divorce his wife if I stayed with him.

I realized that I was neglecting my responsibilities as a mother. If I didn't stop drinking, I'd lose my family again. I'd experienced this pain once before and I wasn't going to again. I made the decision to stop drinking for good. The next day I walked down the highway and told him I couldn't be around him anymore because I was going down the tubes again with my drinking. That was the last time I saw him and the last time I ever drank.

My children were the most important thing in my life, but my drinking was destroying it. I couldn't stop. Today I'm thankful for finally stopping and I'm proud of my son for sharing his story. I'm praying that our story will help others avoid the pain we had to endure.

—*Mom*

Thank you, Mom, for sharing your story, and thank you for your courageous decision to stop drinking. I am the man I am today because of your decision to be healthy for me. I love you!

Let's fast forward to that night I was in jail. With anger in my heart, I blamed my wife for putting me there. I took no responsibility for my own actions. Against the advice of the Domestic Violence (DV) center, she bailed me out. As part of my sentencing I was required to attend weekly DV classes.

I continued attending DV classes for nearly a year and a half but they weren't helping. I continued abusing my wife. As much as I tried, I couldn't stop. To protect herself my wife began abandoning me emotionally and spiritually. I was married but all alone. I was living in shame and the little voice inside my head saying, "You are a monster; you'll never change," constantly plagued my thoughts.

My pain reached a breaking point. Change was *guaranteed*. God had put a counselor in our lives, and he recommended a separation. Just like my mom had left us so that she could get healthy, I left my daughter so that I could get healthy. And just like Mom, this was the level of pain necessary to finally begin the long process of changing me.

I worked for Honeywell (formerly Sundstrand) at the time, and God had surrounded me with a number of godly men. In my wildest dreams, I never thought I'd share my dire situation with them. They knew me as the model employee and the rising star at Honeywell. If they really knew me, they would certainly judge me, and it would impact my career.

I couldn't have been more wrong. The pain of being alone was so great that I humbled myself enough to ask for their help. Bob was one of those men. I'd always admired Bob for how positive he always was, his energy level, and his natural gifts of encouragement. A few years earlier, I'd actually gone with Bob into a prison to preach the gospel to the inmates. I knew Bob was a Christian and I'd watched him from a distance since I'd started work there ten years earlier.

Deciding to take a chance, I asked Bob if he had time to talk, and he offered to take me out for a Coke some time. I'm not sure of the exact date, but I remember the conversation. I shared with Bob that I was separated from my wife. I watched closely, fully expecting a judgmental response.

Instead of judgment, he offered compassion, saying he was sorry and offered to help in any way he could. His compassion and offer to help created a small opening in my heart, enough of an opening that I decided to take a big risk.

"Bob, I have more to tell you. We are separated because I've abused her multiple times, and I haven't been able to stop."

I watched closely to see Bob's response. Once again, there was no hint of judgment. Instead, he said, "We all sin." His past wasn't perfect either. Bob was safe. I could trust him. For the first time in my life, I didn't feel *alone*. I didn't realize it at the time, but God would ultimately use Bob as a primary force in my transformation.

After our conversation, Bob began calling me very regularly. "Hey, Damon, I've been praying for you and thinking about you. I'm just calling to ask how you're doing. Let's go out and grab a Coke again soon."

After a couple of these calls, I decided that he was genuine in his intentions, and I took him up on the offer. Today, Bob is one of my best friends, and I'll be forever grateful for his role in my life.

God put another man from Honeywell (Sundstrand) in my life year's earlier. As a junior in college, I decided it was time to find an internship. On a whim, I went to the career center at the University of Washington and began looking at the opportunities. Unfortunately, it was late in the summer and there was only 1 opportunity. Sundstrand had an internship. I was able to decipher the signature of the hiring manager and took a chance. I called and asked to talk with the hiring manager. He invited me in to talk with Steve, one of the engineers on his team.

My interview with Steve went smoothly, and he recommended hiring me, and so began my professional career. During the interview, I noticed Steve had a Bible on his desk. I wasn't a Christian at the time, but this subtle but visible representation of his faith left an imprint on me. Little did I know at the time, but Steve and his wife Sue would ultimately play a major role in my transformation.

I don't recall the day, but it was only a few weeks after I'd separated from my wife. Sitting at my desk, I struggled to focus on work, consumed with the pain I was experiencing. Steve happened to sit about 4 offices down from me and had a door on his office so he could talk in private. I was in pain so I took a risk.

"Steve, do you have a minute to talk?"

Immediately, Steve dropped everything and diverted his focus to me. "Of course, please come in."

We closed the door and I proceeded to share my situation. I had sensed that I could trust Steve, but I still wasn't sure. I watched him closely as I shared that I was separated. His response was very similar to Bob's.

"Oh, Damon, I'm so sorry." He didn't judge me, he didn't reprimand me. He just expressed his compassion. Steve was a very busy man and I'm certain he didn't have time for me, but I was in deep pain and I needed help.

"Steve, I've got something more to share." I watched

intently to see if he was open to continuing the conversation.

"Please share, Damon. I've got all day."

"Steve, we're separated because I've committed acts of violence against my wife and I haven't been able to change." Once again, I watched him intently to see if he would judge me.

"Thanks for sharing that, Damon. I can't tell you the number of times that I've been angry with my wife in an argument. It's only by the grace of God that I haven't done the same thing."

I was floored. This deep, dark secret that I had was exposed to the light, and by exposing it to the light, it lost its power. God knew what I needed years before I needed it. When my pain was so great, God availed these men to me.

Over the next few months, both Bob and Steve acted as my lifeline. I can't tell you the number of times I went into Steve's office in tears or the number of times that I poured my heart out to Bob driving down the road in his Suburban. I can tell you, however, that through my confession of sin to them, I experienced their forgiveness and they reminded me that Christ had forgiven me.

Eventually, I fully accepted and embraced this forgiveness, and I ultimately forgave myself. James 5:16 makes us this promise, and I experienced it firsthand:

Therefore, confess your sins to one another, and pray for one another so that you may be healed. The effective prayer of a righteous man can accomplish much.

But their support for me went well beyond listening and praying for me. When my wife was granted a protection order to prevent me from being able to transport my daughter, Monica, they were there for me. Every single time, they were there for me. When my house in South Seattle sold and I didn't know where I was going to live, Steve opened his home to me, and I lived in the unfinished room off of his garage for the next 3 months.

When I left Steve's house, Bob let me park my motorhome in his backyard, and I lived there for the next 3 months. God had put these men in my life. They carried me through the hardest times of my life. Through their faith and example, they introduced me to a Jesus I had never known. Through them, I learned to accept Jesus' forgiveness, and I began trusting Him with my life.

Mark tells a story in Chapter 2 that summarizes how Jesus used these 2 men in my life. He shares that 4 men carried a paralyzed man to see Jesus. When the crowds were too great to get to Jesus, they persevered to the point of tearing the roof off the house and lowering the paralyzed man to Jesus.

Jesus responded and after seeing their faith, the man's sins were forgiven.

As I sit here writing this, I am reminded that I am the man I am today because of Steve and Bob's faith and persistence in bringing me to Jesus.

With Steve and Bob in my life I was no longer alone and I was on my way to being healthy. At the time I had no idea how much more pain I'd have to endure to become who He wanted me to be, but God knew.

Questions to Consider

- Have you experienced the principle of *pain drives change* in your life, when the pain of changing was less than the pain of staying the same?
  - Did you choose joy and grow from the pain?
- Who are the Steve's and Bob's in your life?
  - Have you taken a risk and confessed your sin to them?
- If you don't have a Steve or Bob in your life today, who are the people that God is preparing to play their role?
  - How can you proactively develop a friendship with them?
- If you have experienced pain as a child, how has it affected the person you are today?
- How can I help you?
  - You can find more resources and my contact information at **www.paindriveschange.com**.

2
The Pain of Hopelessness

Where there is no vision the people perish...
—Proverbs 29:18

Growing up, I never experienced a home with a "healthy" family. As I mentioned earlier, Mom and Dad divorced when I was only a few years old. Mom struggled with alcoholism, and Dad remarried and started a new family of his own. At the age of 8, my whole family went in different directions while Mom began her recovery from alcoholism. I personally entered a foster home with a married couple, we'll call them the Jones', but they certainly weren't healthy.

My strongest memories of Mrs. Jones came one cool summer evening. She was grossly overweight, and she told me her feet hurt from standing on them all day. She asked me to sit at her feet and rub lotion into her feet to make them feel better.

Who was I, an 8-year-old boy, to say no? As I was sitting on the floor with her feet propped up in the Lazy Boy chair, I began rubbing lotion into her feet. She was clearly enjoying this...as a foster mom, the state was paying her to watch me, and she was getting a foot massage to boot!

The doorbell rang, and she asked Mr. Jones to answer it. I could see the door from my position on the floor under her feet and glanced up to see who it was.

When the door opened, I was elated to see my mom! She had just gotten back to Wenatchee and she wanted to see me. I jumped up to give her a hug and tell her how much I missed her, but I wasn't allowed to.

Mrs. Jones looked at my mom and in a firm tone of voice said, "He's busy right now; you'll have to come back later."

I'll never forget the look on Mom's face. She was crushed and so was I.

The home that she had entrusted her son to had just told her that he was too busy massaging her fat feet and couldn't see her. Mom was livid. This would be the first and last time. Within a couple of days I was transferred to a boys' home in the small town of Manson, Washington.

I'd been in the boys' home for nearly a year when Mom came to work there. She continued to work there while I stayed through my fourth grade year. By the beginning of my fifth grade year, Mom was fully on her feet, and we moved to Grand Coulee, where I lived until I graduated from high school. As a boy in third and fourth grades, I loved staying at the boys' home, and I thought it was a healthy environment. My intuition told me that something wasn't quite right, but it wasn't until my seventh grade year when the FBI came to my school that I learned how wrong things were. I'll share more about this later.

When I met my first wife, I honestly had no intention of marrying her. She had 2 children of her own and their fathers weren't in their lives. After our first date, I met her children, both under ten at the time. We camped, snow skied, rode go-carts, and went sledding together. I read to them before they went to bed and snuggled with them watching Saturday morning cartoons.

This was the family I'd never had! Being with them gave my life purpose! Their dads weren't in their lives and they were as hungry for real family as I was. The dream of family infected their mother and me so deeply that we ignored our own unhealthiness and all of the warning signs. Less than a year after we started dating, we were married. The dream of being a family rapidly turned into a nightmare.

The girls watched helplessly as their mom and I argued. Our home became a war zone. Instead of a safe place where the girls could grow up into healthy young women, it was a place where they watched us destroy each other.

But the dream was embedded deep in my heart and I wouldn't give up. We decided we would bring another life into the world, so on September 27, 1997, my precious baby girl, Monica, was born. In the first few weeks of her life, it felt like our dream for a family was finally coming true. The joy of a newborn child is so powerful that it temporarily lulled us away from the problems that had plagued our marriage. But those problems revealed themselves only a few short weeks later when I found myself in handcuffs and being taken away to the King County Jail.

The dream of family for someone that never had family was so deeply embedded in my soul that I wouldn't let it go. My wife ignored the advice of the DV advocates. With an eye blackened from my blow, she came to King County Jail and bailed me out. Her dream of family was so deep that she, too, would stop at nothing to realize it.

Things didn't get better; they got worse. Part of my sentencing was mandatory DV classes. Every Tuesday night I was required to attend DV classes with a group of 8 to twelve other men that were also required to attend. This class was a low point of my week. Not only did I have to go there, I also had no idea of how long I'd have to be there. When I asked my counselor how long I'd be required to go, he said, "until you're ready to graduate."

Fourteen months later, though, I hadn't gotten better. I was still attending the class and becoming more and more resentful for my time there. My relationship with my wife was worse than ever. My acts of DV didn't stop, and I could feel the pressure building up. Every time that an act of violence occurred, I was required to report it to the class. Reporting it only meant that I would be sentenced to more time of Tuesday nights sitting around listening to men gripe and moan and blame everyone else in their lives for their problems.

I was losing hope that I'd ever improve, and it was pretty obvious that attending DV class wasn't helping. Furthermore, my wife's actions indicated that she, too, had given up on me and our marriage. I won't speak poorly of her and her actions in this book. As the man of this home and family, today I take 100% responsibility for my actions. I don't blame her for how she responded to the problems in our marriage. However, it was clear to my DV counselor and the men in my class that, if something didn't change quickly, I would find myself in jail again. The pain of hopelessness for my marriage and hopelessness that I'd ever get healthy was so great that something was going to change—it was guaranteed.

On January 8, 1999, the pain finally drove a change. I had to let go of the dream for family, which I'd held so deeply in my heart for my whole life. The pain of moving out and abandoning my dream was less than the pain of living in an abusive marriage. This was the hardest thing I ever had to do. I was abandoning my child and my family just as I had been abandoned as an 8-year-old boy.

As long as I live, the imprint of fifteen-month-old Monica standing at the window of our home waving "goodbye Daddy" will never leave me. My hope for her to never experience growing up without a mom and dad as I had turned into hopelessness as I drove away that dark, rainy night.

Years earlier, in a slightly manic episode of my life, I

decided to buy a little red house in the slums of Seattle. I rented this house out for years. My friends called me a "slum lord." A month earlier, my tenant had moved out and this was the only place I could go. I had no friends to stay with, so I decided I'd live there until things got better in our marriage or we divorced, which ever came first.

The pouring rain concealed the tears that rolled down my face as I unpacked a few things from my truck and moved them into this place.

I wept uncontrollably for what seemed like hours that evening, wanting nothing more than to go to sleep so I didn't have to feel the pain. But sleep doesn't come easily when you are weeping. I got on my knees and I pleaded with God to take the pain away, to make everything okay. I pleaded with Him to be the father to Monica and my 2 stepdaughters that I couldn't be. I begged Him to heal our marriage, to heal me of my DV issues, and restore our marriage. The tears didn't stop, but I found comfort in crying out to God.

I finally fell asleep that night, but my sleep didn't bring me rest. Nightmares of being abandoned as a child overwhelmed my sleep. Fears of never reconciling with my wife penetrated my soul. When morning came, I couldn't bear the thought of getting up and being all alone in this small house in South Seattle. Sleep was the only comfort I could find from this pain. But sleep didn't come, and eventually I had to get up.

My days were filled with hopelessness. I wanted desperately to believe that this wasn't real. I remember calling my wife on the phone, looking to her to provide me hope for our future. But she didn't. Our conversations quickly turned to arguments ending with a "click" as the phone was hung up.

At least I had my work to escape to. Things were great at work. My small team of engineers was awesome. I found a lot of joy in leading them to results. At least I had my work...

Only a few days later I, was informed that my small team of engineers was being reorganized and that I would no longer be a manager. I, too, was being re-organized as an individual contributor, doing detailed mechanical engineering design. I'm not a detailed person, and detailed mechanical engineering work was drudgery to me. I always dreaded it when it came up, and now my days would be filled with it. The hope I received in coming to work to manage a high-performing team was instantly transformed into the hopelessness of detail drudgery.

I didn't want to go to my new home and be all alone with myself. I didn't want to come to work and be alone. Going to my old home with my family wasn't a viable option because it would only bring deeper pain through the fighting and arguments, and an even deeper pain when I had to leave my daughter.

I really had no way of escaping my pain and I found myself getting more and more hopeless as the days went by. I continued pleading with God and always found temporary relief during these times.

On January 13, 1999, just 5 days after my separation, I began a process that would eventually become the inspiration for this book. I placed my video camera on a tripod and began a video diary.

The first night I replayed the story that had gotten me to this place. More than thirty minutes later, I had finished my story up to that point, and I committed myself to continuing the process so that I could reflect and embed the things I was learning in my counseling sessions and in my life.

That first night of video journaling recorded a few signs of hope. I had no idea at the time, but God was planting the seeds to transform me into the man I am today. I reported that my counselor suspected that I was depressed and recommended

I visit my doctor to get on some anti-depressants.

I noted that a few days earlier, I had been listening to the radio and heard Dr. Jim Talley talk about his book, *Reconcilable Differences*, outlining a process to help couples in our situation to reconcile. I shared that I began experiencing peace without the chaos of being at home and fighting with my wife.

After only 5 days of being separated, I was transforming hopelessness into hope. God heard my cry and was with me even when I didn't feel Him, and He was making the way for the deepest areas of my unhealthiness to be healed.

I waited patiently for the LORD; he turned to me and heard my cry. He lifted me out of the slimy pit, out of the mud and mire; he set my feet on a rock and gave me a firm place to stand. He put a new song in my mouth, a hymn of praise to our God. Many will see and fear the LORD and put their trust in him.   —Psalm 40:1-3

God was lifting me out of the slimy pit of DV and was in the process of giving me a firm place to stand. After being in DV class for nearly a year, I remember asking myself, "Why am I not getting any better?" It felt like there was a cycle to my moods and my DV episodes.

I got up the courage to ask for a meeting with my DV counselor. I asked him how I was doing and if I'd ever graduate. He told me I had a long way to go and that by asking him when I'd graduate and what it would take to graduate indicated that I was still trying to control my life. Until I could let go of that control, I wouldn't graduate.

This, of course, gave me less hope and made me angry, but he was right. The need to be in control is one of the symptoms of a person struggling with DV. When the situation gets out of control, a person struggling with DV resorts to physical violence to regain control. This was my pattern as well.

I asked the counselor how bad my emotional health was as it related to DV. He shared that I was so unhealthy that I was lower than his standard scale of 1-10, with 1 being extremely unhealthy and 10 being extremely healthy. He said, "You are a negative 4 on this scale. I've never seen anyone as unhealthy as you are."

Emotional health

Wow! Instead of offering me hope, I again was crushed and filled with hopelessness. I finally told him that I felt like my moods cycled and had been wondering if I had a form of bipolar disease.

He was too quick to respond, saying that I certainly wasn't bipolar, and that by even thinking I might be indicated I wasn't taking responsibility for my moods and actions.

Fortunately, he wasn't the only counselor in my life.

> *Without consultation, plans are frustrated,*
> *but with many counselors they succeed.*
> —Proverbs 15:22

My marriage counselor noticed that I was severely depressed and recommended that I see my primary physician. Only a few short days after my wife and I separated, I took his advice and visited my primary care physician, the same doctor who had delivered Monica. I shared with him my struggles with hopelessness. I courageously opened up with him and shared my struggles with DV.

His response changed my life forever. He said that I was depressed, but there was more. My marriage counselor had suspected I might be bipolar, and after hearing my struggles, he agreed. His diagnosis was that I had Cyclothymia and drew this graph for me.

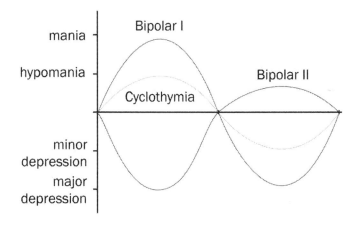

He shared that Cyclothymia was a mild form of bipolar disorder. Furthermore, he said that the cause of bipolar is genetic, and my struggles with depression weren't because I was crazy or weak or a bad person, they were biological. Stated differently, my depression was not something I could willfully control. My depression was a part of my body's bipolar cycle, and that we would have to work together to identify the right combination of medicine to get me out of depression. He shared that it would be a journey of discovery and it might take time. He also shared that we needed to be very cautious because too much medicine could trigger the other side of my bipolar, hypomania, and perhaps mania.

I didn't understand what *mania* meant, so I asked him to explain. He told me that when people are hypomanic or manic there are a number of signs: lots of energy, poor sleep, spending excessive amounts of money, being hypersexual, and irritability with fits of rage. Finally, he shared that DV was common for people with bipolar.

Thoughts raced through my mind. I regularly experienced all the symptoms he'd outlined. *Could this be the reason I wasn't improving with my DV? Could this explain why there were times in my life when I had incredible amounts of energy and did crazy things, and other times I was so lethargic that I couldn't even get out of bed? Could this explain why I had committed multiple acts of DV?*

So I asked him the big question: *Was this the cause of my DV?* He was reluctant to say that it was the only cause, but he did share a little bit of the chemistry of bipolar. I'm not a doctor, but I'll try to summarize what he said. He said that in people without bipolar, there is a chemical that enables a "pause" between stimulus and response, but this chemical response doesn't occur in people that are bipolar. Stated differently, the bipolar brain triggers immediate reaction to a stimulus.

Bipolar

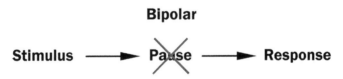

I reflected on the times of DV and remembered how I never felt like I had control in the instant it happened. My acts of DV were characterized by an instant physical response in the heat of an argument. *Was this discovery the hope that I'd been looking for? Was this the path that would ensure that I'd never commit the horrific acts of violence again?*

My doctor prescribed an antidepressant and a drug called Depakote. He said that the antidepressant would bring me out of my depression and that the Depakote would "smooth out" my cycles. Furthermore, Depakote works quite well because it creates the "pause" between stimulus and response. He mentioned that if I tracked my moods, we could refine the medicines, and I might eventually experience a life without the highs and lows that are driven by being bipolar. Finally, he shared that many people struggle with the medication and stop taking it because they no longer experience the euphoria when they are experiencing hypomania and mania.

I promised him I would take my medication in the exact doses he recommended; I would also track my moods. Years later, he told me that he'd never had a patient as diligent and responsible as I was in managing my bipolar disorder.

I began taking my medication immediately after that visit, and it gradually started lifting me out of depression. Not only that, but I was able to control my impulses. I found myself able to pull back from arguing with my wife. *I'm proud to say that I have never been physically abusive since the day I began taking this medication!*

I was now on a path to being healthy, and I could feel the momentum building. During one of my video journals in late January, I reported that I was feeling good about myself and that I no longer had the little voice in my head telling me that I was a monster. I was no longer acting like a victim but was proactively doing what needed to be done to become the man God wanted me to be.

I shared that I didn't want to visit my old house anymore where my wife and kids lived. I had discovered that my heart would race when I arrived. Furthermore, multiple triggers happened while I was there.

I was growing and my wife wasn't. She began looking for things that I was doing wrong so that she could justify her own wrongs. On another video journal, I said that I felt like

I needed to stop going to the house, and I needed to stop seeing her for a while.

God has an interesting way of giving us what we need. On the day after Valentine's Day, I went to the house to pick Monica up for a short visit. My wife said something that triggered a response. In a firm but non-aggressive tone, I assertively stated my feelings in a way that I had been counseled to do so. I told her I was tired of being used. I was tired of paying all the bills and doing all of the driving to see my daughter. I told her I was tired of being blamed for all of the problems in our marriage, and I was tired of how she treated me.

She didn't like this, so she threatened to call the police. I was angry, but I knew I wasn't in the wrong. I knew that there wouldn't be any violence, so I told her, "Go ahead and call the police; I've done nothing wrong."

Her older daughter saw that her mom wasn't able to push my buttons and was angry with me because I'd told her earlier that her twenty-year-old boyfriend (she was fifteen at the time) couldn't stay at the house with her. She began verbally attacking me just as her mom had done so many times in the past.

My response to her was the same as my response to her mom. I assertively told her that I was tired of being used and tired of being treated so poorly.

I left the house that evening and I happened to have my DV group. I told them and the counselor what I'd done, and they praised me for being assertive and for sharing my feelings—but also for being wise enough to leave the house.

I was exuberant about my personal victory. On my video journal that night, I said that what I had done was what healthy people do in healthy relationships. I described my feelings and set some personal boundaries. I was going to talk with our marriage counselor about not seeing my wife for a while and not going to the house again. I was ready to really focus on improving myself.

My marriage counselor had told me that something would change in my relationship with my wife. He believed that I was making enormous progress, and because of this progress, my wife was feeling pressured to make progress or find an excuse not to. He was right.

The next night there was a knock on my door, and I was handed an envelope. I opened the envelope to find a protection order against me. My wife had been granted a protection order that made it illegal for me to visit the house and illegal for me to contact her outside of marriage counseling or written letters. If I chose to ignore the protection order, I'd find myself in jail.

Pain drives change. God knew what I needed, and I knew what I needed. The protection order was His tool to make it happen.

The order was His way of giving me what I needed at the time, and the consequences of not following it were so painful that my personal adherence to that piece of paper would be easy. The stove had burned my hand so many times in the past that I didn't need to put my hand on it again to know that it would hurt. I now had a reason to focus on myself and get healthy.

At our next counseling appointment, my wife stated that she wanted to find a new counselor for herself and also wanted to decrease the frequency of our marriage counseling to monthly. We agreed to make the change.

In only a few short weeks, God had given me hope when I was hopeless. The discovery that I had bipolar disorder, the medicine, combined with the protection order, and minimized interactions with my wife, were catalysts that would enable incredible growth in me.

God had placed my feet upon a rock and now I had a firm place to stand. A few weeks later, He would put a new song in my mouth, but once again, I would need to experience some pain to drive the next level of change.

Questions to Consider

- Do you ever find yourself struggling with depression?
  - If so, what were the circumstances?
  - How did you overcome it?
- Do you ever find yourself euphoric for extended periods of time (for example, not needing sleep, excessive spending, being irritable, or hypersexual)?
  - If so, what were the circumstances?
  - How did you overcome it?
- Have you experienced separation for the purposes of personal growth in any of your relationships?
  - How did you respond?
  - What was the result?
- Are you in pain?
  - If so, what needs to happen so that you will trust God and find joy in it so that He can change you for the better?
- How can I help you?
  - You can find more resources and my contact information at **www.paindriveschange.com**.

3
The Joy of a Dream and Vision

Then the LORD answered me and said, "Record the vision and inscribe it on tablets, that the one who reads it may run."
—Habakkuk 2:2

They served me with the protection order on February 16, 1999. I was in shock when I received it, but I felt a strange sense of relief. I could no longer visit the house that I'd personally remodeled a few years before I was married. I could no longer see my wife, which, ironically, meant that I was protected from her verbal assaults and attacks on my personal character. I could no longer put my daughter to bed in her own crib, so I wouldn't feel the pain of leaving her at night.

The relief quickly turned to anger and pain. I could no longer call my wife on the phone when I needed encouragement or the hope that things would be all right. Strangely enough, we would randomly have very pleasant conversations that would give me brief glimpses of hope. Only a few weeks earlier, we had one of those glimpses. We shared a pleasant conversation on the phone and enjoyed each other's company at church, followed by a pleasant meal as a family at a restaurant.

I shared on my video journal how good it felt to be treated kindly, and how I missed my wife and family. I even shared my excitement with my DV group. They looked at me like I was crazy. How did 2 days of peace erase my memories of two and a half years of constant fighting? They were right. That brief glimpse of hope was shattered during another phone call. She attacked me and began defending her actions that were destroying any remnant of trust we had in each other.

A mentor of mine taught me something I'll never forget. He asked me if I knew why gambling was addicting. I didn't know, so he told me. He said that gambling is addicting because the reward is random. The random reward of winning money is so euphoric that it keeps you losing money time after time after time with the hope of winning. I was addicted to the random reward of her approval, and it would take me years of pain to finally free myself from this cycle and the need for her approval.

The protection order was actually protecting me! It clearly spelled out the days and times that I could visit Monica. However, my rights as a father to fulfill the most important duty in my life had been instantly stripped away. I could have "visitation" with my own baby girl. God doesn't ask fathers to "visit" their kids, He commands us to protect them and raise them up in the fear of the Lord. Needless to say, I was enraged, but I could do nothing about it.

There are consequences to sin, and I was beginning to experience them. DV is ugly. It destroys marriages and it destroys families, but those affected by it need protection, and I fully support their decision in granting her the protection order. Now I was experiencing the consequences, the greatest of which was losing my rights as a father.

As I mentioned earlier, people struggling with DV need to control everything in their lives. God needed to eliminate my need for control to heal me of DV, so He used the law as a form of discipline to put me in a situation that was completely out of my control. I didn't know it at the time, but I would need another two and a half years of agonizing emotional pain to finally let go of control and trust Him with my life.

All discipline for the moment seems not to be joyful, but sorrowful; yet to those who have been trained by it, afterwards it yields the peaceful fruit of righteousness.
—Hebrews 12:11

How was I going to pick Monica up and drop her off? A few days after I was served with the protection order, I humbled myself again and asked Bob for help. As he always does, he said yes. His willingness to help deepened my trust in him.

I parked my car at a gas station near my house. Bob met me there, and while I waited, he drove to the house and picked Monica up and brought her to me. I needed to go to the bank, so I asked Bob if I could ride with him to the bank. As we pulled up to the teller window, I looked in the rearview mirror and saw my wife and her 2 girls.

My heart started racing and I was flooded with fear. The protection order didn't allow me to be within 200 yards of her. Not realizing it was Bob, she had pulled up right behind him. I was now at great risk and was violating the protection order. Bob pulled forward and parked, asking her to do the same. He asked me to stay in the car while he went and talked with her. The girls got out of the car and came over to talk with me.

"Why don't you come to the house anymore?" they asked. They were feeling like I'd abandoned them. I told them their mom had gotten a protection order and that I wouldn't be going to the house anymore. I also told them I couldn't talk with them right now because the protection order wouldn't allow me to be within 200 yards of them, either. Of course, they didn't understand, but they obeyed me when I told them to go back to their car.

They were now experiencing the consequences of my sin as I abandoned them to protect myself. Very soon afterward, their pain from this abandonment would drive them to change, but the ways in which they changed would only make their lives worse.

Bob came back to his Suburban and told me not to worry that he had made the decision to talk with her, and he would personally take any consequences from the law if it came to that. He was protecting me.

My visit with Monica was extremely challenging. I was experiencing so much joy with her that I feared the pain I'd feel when she had to go home. Bob took her home, and I went back to my house in South Seattle. I cried my eyes out for what seemed to be an eternity, missing my daughter, longing to snuggle with her and rock her to sleep, but I couldn't.

The pain of missing her was so great that I contemplated not seeing her so that I wouldn't have to experience this pain. For the first time in my life, I felt some empathy for why my own father rarely visited me. He, too, was avoiding this pain.

On Sunday, February 28, I drove Monica to the first of 3 church services I attended on Sundays. Our time at church was really the only time that I fully experienced peace, so I took advantage of it. Our first service was held in a movie theatre in Woodinville (the town where I currently live). Monica would sit on my lap during church, snuggling with me. I don't remember the message, but I do remember feeling very emotional. Tears flowed.

Monica said, "Daddy, why are you crying?"

"Because I love you and miss you, honey."

I've never audibly heard God's voice, but I regularly hear His voice in my head directing me and guiding me. On this day, I vividly remember what He said.

"Damon, you need a vision and some goals in your life."

"Okay," I thought, and while I agreed, I didn't know how

to set goals and I certainly didn't have vision past that day. Who do I know that can help, I thought? "Bob! Bob is the most goal-oriented person I knew. I would ask Bob!"

It turned out that Bob attended the church where I went to my second service. I drove there and sat with Bob and his 7 children while we worshipped and listened to the Word. Afterwards, I asked Bob if he could help me with goals.

"Sure," he said. "Why don't you come over to our house and we'll do it today? Monica can play with my kids while we have lunch together and work on it."

"Sure," I said.

I remember going to his house and watching his kids play. I remember the peace that I experienced sitting on his couch. Where was the fighting and arguing? This wasn't normal. Certainly, the kids would be fighting with each other, and their mom would be yelling at them telling them to stop. But I didn't see it. I saw laughter and playing. I saw them treating Monica like she was their own sister. I watched them work together in the kitchen making lunch, and I saw them all sit at the table together for lunch. I watched Bob pray for the meal and everyone respectfully waiting their turn to get their food.

Never in my life had I experienced a family that acted this way. This is weird, I thought. They must not be normal.

"Damon, this is normal. God is good. Let's go downstairs and start working on your goals. Damon, from now on, DV doesn't stand for domestic violence. It stands for dream and vision. Vision is more caught than taught, you need to spend time in environments where you can catch a vision for your life."

Bob was right. In the few brief hours I'd spent with his family, I caught a vision for what "healthy family" looked like. I caught the vision for what I wanted *my* life and family to look like.

Bob then asked me to open my Bible and read Habakkuk 2:2-4:

Then the LORD answered me and said: "Record the vision And inscribe it on tablets, so that one who reads it may run. For the vision is yet for the appointed time; It hastens toward the goal and it will not fail. Though it tarries, wait for it; For it will certainly come, it will not delay."

Bob then told me about a study by Harvard that validates the scripture above.

"Studies at Harvard and Yale Universities have tracked the results of goal-setting. They surveyed people at graduation and found that 3% of the graduates had written goals and strategies for achieving them, 10% had goals in mind, but no written strategies, 60% had wishes and dreams, and 27% didn't have a clue. Twenty years later, the surviving members of the classes demonstrated the awesome power of written goals: the 3% who had written goals were worth more than the other 97% combined."

"Damon, it's time to write some goals down. It's time to take Monica home, so how about if I take her home and you stay here and write out a dream for your life? Make it extremely vivid with great detail. Don't constrain yourself to where you are today in your life. Dream big; have fun. God is good!"

As I buckled her into the car seat in Bob's Suburban, I hugged Monica and told her I loved her and would see her soon.

"Daddy, I don't want to go. I love you." Her beautiful brown eyes filled with tears. I kissed her and said goodbye, assuring her that it would be okay. Once again, she waved goodbye as Bob drove away. I felt the same emotions I'd felt 7 weeks earlier when I drove away, overcome with tears.

Truth be told, I didn't think it would be okay. I hated saying goodbye to my little girl. Why should she have to suffer because of my sin? Why should she have to be separated from me because her mom and I couldn't make it work? She didn't deserve this.

On that day, I vowed to do everything in my power to stop the generational curses that had plagued my family. I would become healthy, and I would stop the power of addiction in my own life and my family's life. Monica would not suffer as I had suffered. She would never experience the pain of being without a father in her life, and she would never have a hole in her heart like I did. The pain of my daughter's tears would fuel the changes that I needed to make.

I walked back into Bob's home office and took his advice to write my dream. The words flowed from my hands as I wrote my dream. The words below are exactly what I wrote.

My Dream

My dream is to have a Christian family. We live in a small town with clean streets and sidewalks. The sun is out, and I'm playing catch with my children in the yard. The 100-year-old shade tree shades our home. My wife calls us in for dinner, and we pray together at the table. We enjoy our dinner and talk about our day. Everyone is smiling, and you can feel the love in the air. After dinner, I do the dishes with the children. We go into the living room and play games until bedtime. I put the children to bed, and my wife and I pray with them. When we wake up, breakfast is on the table and we all start our day together. I go to work, and get home right after the kids do, and we start again. Peace, Love, Joy—these embody my dream.

This was my dream. I'd held this dream in my heart

my whole life, but I'd never written it down. On this day, I wrote the dream as the Lord had told Habakkuk to do. I didn't know how this dream would come true, but I was obedient and wrote it down. The scripture promises that by writing the dream, we will be able to run. This dream unlocked incredible power within me, a power so strong that it virtually eradicated the hopelessness I was feeling. A power that erased my fears of Monica growing up without a dad and a family. A power that only God could provide.

For God hath not given us the spirit of fear,
but of power, and of love, and of a sound mind.
—2 Timothy 1:7

Bob came home and I shared my dream with him. He said, "God is good, Damon. You now have a dream and a vision to replace your DV. Now let's talk about how to fuel this dream."

"Bob, how is it that you always have so much energy?" I asked.

"God is good and He blesses me. Imagine a glass of water. The clear water represents all of the good in our lives. When we look through the glass, we can still see our vision clearly. But now imagine that I take a drop of red dye and put it in the glass. The red dye represents the negative in our lives. What happens?"

"I can't see through the glass anymore; I can't see my vision."

"Exactly," Bob said. "So what can you do to see the vision?"

"Pour it out and start new," I said.

"Nope, can't do it. This water and dye represent your life and all that has happened to you up until that point."

Hmm, I thought. "What about adding more water?"

"Exactly," Bob said. "Now imagine the same amount of red dye, but in a pitcher of water, you can barely notice the dye. What about the same amount of dye in a 5-gallon bucket? A swimming pool? Lake Washington? The ocean? You get the point," he said. "I have so much energy because I fill my life with positives. It's not that there aren't any negatives in my life, it's just that I have so much positive that I can't see the negative."

"How about you, Damon? How much clear water do you have in your life?"

"Not much, Bob. And I have no energy."

Bob went to his whiteboard and drew a line down the middle. On the left, he wrote "Negatives" and on the right, he wrote "Positives." Let's start with the negatives.

Negatives	Positives
• Domestic Violence	• Bob
• Separated from family	• Steve
• Depressed	• Pat & Manfred
• Bipolar	• Marriage Counselor
• Work not satisfying	• Church
• No extra money	• I'm physical healthy
• Wife not working toward reconciling marriage	• Meds seem to be helping with bipolar and depression
• Dad not in my life	• I'm smart
• I miss Monica	• I can see God's hand in my life
• Monica growing up without dad	• Protection order is keeping me from relapsing
• Protection order	• Monica
• House is selling, no place to live	• Video journaling
• Stepdaughters starting to rebel	
• Boss says I'm a loose cannon at work and doesn't know what to do with me	
• Counseling is costing more money than I have	
• My cat just died	
• My dog doesn't have a place to live	
• I'm angry with my mom for all she did to me	
• Where I live is dangerous	
• DV class is draining me emotionally	

I was shocked at how many negatives I had in my life, and it helped me understand why I never had any energy.

"OK," Bob said. "Here's the good news. The negatives provide you with the motivation to change, and you have a lot of positives in your life. Let's prioritize the negatives and set goals to turn them into positives."

That was easy. "Missing Monica and her growing up without a dad in her life were the most important things to change, and changing them would align directly with my new dream," I said.

"How about setting a goal to maximize every opportunity I have with her?" I asked.

"That's good, but it's not a goal, Damon. A good goal needs to be specific, measurable, achievable, realistic, and timely. S.M.A.R.T."

"Okay."

Here are some of the goals I wrote down for my family:

Family

- Dinner 1x/week with strong Christian families
- Continue personal counseling 1x/week
- Continue marriage counseling
- Finish *Growing Kids God's Way* by April 1
- Pray with Monica before each meal and before bedtime
- Pray for my wife every night before I go to bed
- Spend 100% of my visitation time with Monica

"Before we continue, let me teach you some scripture. Don't dwell on the negatives in your life, but focus on the positives," Bob said.

Finally, brethren, whatever is true, whatever is honorable, whatever is right, whatever is pure, whatever is lovely, whatever is of good repute, if there is any excellence and if anything worthy of praise, dwell on these things.
—Philippians 4:8

"I want you to put your goals in a place where you can see them every day and I want you to read them. I want you to read your dream out loud every day as well," Bob told me.

"OK," I said, "I'll do it."

"Before we establish more goals, I want to teach you another concept. I call it *Unifying Life Principles (ULPs)*. Imagine that you had the ability to watch your own funeral.

What words would you want people to use to describe you? Let's pull out some yellow sticky notes and write yours down," Bob said.

| Abide by God's Principles | Be a Man of Integrity | Honor my Wife |
| Commit to Worthy Goals | Enjoy High Self-Esteem | Be a Highly Effective Father |

"Now we need to prioritize them and describe what each means. Take a few minutes and do that."

Below are the unifying life principles I wrote that day. As I was prioritizing them, it occurred to me that the one area of my life that I was the strongest in and had always excelled in was the least important thing to me—my work! If I wanted to become this man I'd have to re-prioritize where I focused my energy.

- **Be a Man of Integrity**. All my actions seek to edify and honor God and God's word. My words and actions seek the truth.

- **Abide by God's Principles**. My life principles are based on God's precepts. Strive to honor God with my actions and words. Seek God's counsel during times of trouble. Always, always, always do the right thing.

- **Commit to Worthy Goals**. "Without a vision the people perish." Establish long-range, intermediate-range, and daily goals. Focus on achieving these, often at the expense of "more interesting" things. Be passionate in all that I do.

- **Enjoy High Self-Esteem**. Love myself. Pursue activities and relationships in my life that will build me up, not tear me down.

- **Enjoy Good Health**. Maintain physical and emotional

wellbeing. Avoid things in my life that don't produce fruit. Focus on the positive.

- **Honor My Wife**. "Husbands love your wives as Christ loved the Church." Be the husband that God expects of me. Cherish my wife, and edify her through all my actions and words.

- **Be a Highly Effective Father**. Love and cherish my children through my actions and words. Teach my children to live to the highest level of integrity, honor, and respect. Establish God and God's word as the ultimate authority. Teach my children AGAPE.

- **Love My Extended Family**. Honor my father and mother. Continue to cherish brother and sisters through thick and thin.

- **Care for People**. Consider other's needs as more important than my own. Seek to build others through my actions and words.

- **Establish Financial Security**. Think long term. Maintain financial integrity and responsibility. Seek to honor God and God's work with my tithes and offerings.

- **Give Selflessly**. I was put on this earth to establish relationships. Give of myself to pursue and enable these relationships.

- **Have Fun**. Enjoy life. Work to live, don't live to work.

- **Be a Teacher**. God has given me a life of experiences and abilities. Share them with others. "To teach it is to learn it twice."

- **Be Respected at Work**. Perform my works as to the Lord. My actions and words are with integrity and passion. Servant leadership is fundamental to advancing the kingdom of God.

"By prioritizing these items," Bob said, "you can set goals

to proactively become this person."

Bob shared that it is really easy to know what is important in a person's life. Just look at their checkbook and their calendar. Where people spend their time and money reveals their priorities.

He challenged me to write down some more goals and promised me he would teach me how to proactively schedule my time to accomplish these goals. We proceeded to write out a number of new goals. Each goal that we wrote was intentionally aligned to my ULPs.

"The rest is easy," Bob said. "Fill your time trying to accomplish these goals, and before you know it, there will be so much clear water that you won't even see the red dye."

I followed his advice and proactively focused my time on accomplishing these goals. Bob had shared that the person we will be in 5 years is determined by the people we spend our time with and the books that we read today. I had a vision of who I wanted to be, so I surrounded myself with people that had what I wanted.

I filled my mind and heart with books and tapes to learn how to have that life. I listened to tapes that taught me how to be a better husband and father during my drive times to and from work. I read voraciously and I intentionally spent lots of time with Bob and his family.

God had given me a dream and a vision. Now, I had a plan to achieve it. Whether or not the dream would be fulfilled was largely beyond my control. However, the process to achieve the dream was clear and completely in my control. I no longer had to be a victim of circumstances but could proactively improve myself and my life.

To coin a phrase I often share:

The right process will deliver the right results.
—Toyota

Time would validate the wisdom of this statement. I could focus my efforts on controlling things that were 100% within my control, which freed me to let go of the things that were out of my control.

Questions to Consider

- What is the dream that God has given you?
  - Have you written it down?
- What goals do you have to accomplish this dream?
  - Have you written them down?
- Is there more "red dye" or "clear water" in your life?
  - What do you need to do to change it?
- How can I help you?
  - You can find more resources and my contact information at **www.paindriveschange.com**.

4
The Joy of Congruency

Do not be conformed to this world,
but continuously be transformed by the renewing of your minds
so that you may be able to determine what God's will is
—what is proper, pleasing, and perfect.
—Romans 12:2

Bob equipped me with a new paradigm for life, and he'd given me the most powerful set of tools that I'd ever had. I drove home that night with more hope than I can ever remember experiencing. The little voice that said, "You are a monster, you'll never change" was replaced with a voice of confidence expressing the man God had intended me to be.

"I am a man of integrity." "I am a Godly man." "I am an effective father." "I am a man who loves and honors his wife." "I enjoy self-esteem." "I care deeply for people."

Bob reminded me that by continuously focusing on my new unifying life principles I would eventually be transformed just like Romans 12:2 promises. Furthermore, he taught me about the power of the spoken word:

With the fruit of a man's mouth his stomach will be satisfied;
he will be satisfied with the product of his lips.
Death and life are in the power of the tongue,
and those who love it will eat its fruit.
—Proverbs 18:20-21

He challenged me to verbalize my unifying life principles every day. I must admit, saying them out loud was pretty awkward at first. Fortunately, I lived alone, so nobody heard me! Before I knew it the old voice in my head was gone, but it would take years before my actions would prove that I was no longer that monster. They did, however. As I mentioned earlier, by the grace of God, I haven't committed a single act of DV since my separation.

As the days progressed, I noticed I had more and more energy, just as Bob had promised I would. Marriage counseling, up until this time, was filled with yelling, screaming, and accusations. This all changed. When my wife would express her anger and accuse me of something, I no longer reacted. Instead, the new voice would remind me that honoring my wife meant not yelling at her but listening to her. My counselor was seeing incredible growth in me, but my wife couldn't see it. She was still trapped in her anger towards me.

It became obvious to me and everyone else around me that I was growing, and she was not. When I reflected on the red dye in my life, almost all of it was gone—except for my relationship with my wife. After every interaction with her, I found myself drained of energy and second-guessing myself. Fortunately, the protection order protected me from seeing and talking with her, outside of letters and marriage counseling.

When my phone would ring, I'd check the caller ID to see who was calling. If my caller ID showed that it was my wife, I would instinctively want to answer it. After all, we were married. Sure, there was a protection order, but nobody would know that we'd talked except us. In these moments, I'd hear a little voice in my head saying, "You are a man of integrity. Men of integrity follow the law." I was being transformed just like Romans 12:2 promised, and ignoring the phone calls became easier and easier over time.

Only a few months earlier I'm certain I would have

answered the call. She was my wife and I had a right to talk with her! Not to mention that talking with her offered the hope of making me feel better so I'd certainly answer it. My life before ULPs was characterized by making decisions based on how I felt, and I usually made decisions that would make me feel better momentarily. The long-term impact of these decisions was generally detrimental, but I didn't know any other way.

I never realized how many decisions a couple makes together. Making decisions is hard work and always required enormous emotional energy. After I discovered my unifying life principles, making decisions was easy. I would simply ask, "If I decide to do it this way, is it aligned with my unifying life principles?" I didn't have to spend emotional energy deciding what to do. Men of integrity align their decisions to their unifying life principles. Since being a man of integrity was my number one ULP, my decisions were automatic.

Before ULPs, I spent the majority of my emotional energy making decisions. After ULPs, I found myself with more energy than I'd ever had. As I watch the transition on my video journals, it is amazing to see the difference in my demeanor. I was more positive, hopeful, and energetic. I no longer reflected on the past but focused on the future. My voice was no longer monotonic, but it became animated, filled with passion, and I smiled.

I visited Bob and told him about my newfound energy. We went to his whiteboard and I drew a couple of diagrams that depicted my ability to make decisions.

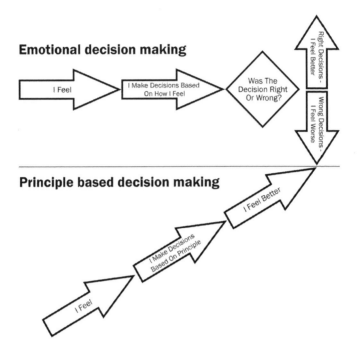

Decisions that are made based on emotion will either make you feel better or worse, depending on how you felt when you made the decision. For example, when my wife asked me to leave the house during an argument, I didn't feel like it. I felt like seeing my daughter, so I ignored her request and stayed, visiting my daughter.

It felt good to visit my daughter, and as her father, I had the right to do so, and I did. After I left the house, however, I didn't feel very good about my decision. I had ignored her request, and in doing so, I damaged the relationship. My emotional decision made me feel better in the moment, but afterwards I felt worse.

Making decisions based on principle makes you feel better. Many times, these decisions are very hard to make in the moment and won't feel good while you're making the decision, but afterwards you will feel better because you have made the decision. For example, when I was alone and feeling depressed, I didn't feel like driving to the house and picking Monica up to spend time with her. I felt like sitting in front of the TV and taking a nap. However, when comparing this decision against my unifying life principle of being an effective father, it was obvious that I needed to spend time with Monica, even though I didn't feel like it. After I picked her up, I found myself feeling better because I'd made my decision based on principle, not emotion. A former pastor summed it up very well: "It's never wrong to do the right thing."

I'm a bit of a geek. I love creating and using simple tools that improve efficiency and effectiveness. One of the tools we used at work in the creation of new products was called a Pugh Concept Selection. This tool is simple but powerful. Compare your design choices against a set of criteria and use these criteria to make a decision. I had an idea: I could build a similar tool for decision making. That was the day I invented the Congruency Matrix.

	Unifying Life Principles													
	A Man of Integrity	Abide by God's Principles	Commit to Worthy Goals	Enjoy High Self Esteem	Enjoy Good Health	Honor my Wife	Be an Effective Father	Love my Extended Family	Care for People	Establish Financial Security	Give Selflessly	Have Fun	Be a Teacher	Total
Stay at house when asked to leave	-	-	0	-	0	-	-	0	-	0	-	0	0	-7
Visit Monica during visitation	+	+	+	+	0	+	+	0	+	0	+	+	+	+10
Domestic Violence	-	-	-	-	-	-	-	-	-	-	-	-	-	-14
Separate from wife and get healthy	+	+	+	+	+	+	+	+	+	+	+	+	+	+14

The Congruency Matrix is a simple tool that transformed my thinking and my actions. Its simplicity allowed me to weigh every decision and goal against my unifying life principles. If this decision or goal was congruent with the specific ULP a "+" would go in the box. If this decision or goal was incongruent, put a "−" in the box. If this decision had no impact on the ULP, put a "0" in the box. Total the values, and the values with the highest total are those decisions or goals that will produce personal congruency.

My life wasn't instantly transformed when I created the congruency matrix. Making congruent decisions and accomplishing congruent goals didn't instantly change me, either. However, every congruent decision made a small improvement in my life and in my character. Decisions made without this framework are decisions made on emotion, and did not result in improvements in my character. Prior to this approach I expected "quick fixes" to my problems, and when there weren't quick fixes, I would get frustrated and stop trying.

Over time, I found my life getting better and better. Slow, incremental improvements were having a compounding effect, and I was becoming the man God created me to be.

We are what we repeatedly do.
Excellence, then, is not an act, but a habit.
—Aristotle

I was enjoying the fruit of my congruent life so much that I wanted to start sharing this approach with others. I'd struggled my whole life without any improvement. Now, the pieces were coming together and I was growing. I was overcoming my issues and people were noticing a change in me.

I don't remember the exact date, but I did talk about it on my video journal: "I think I know what I'm supposed to do with my life. I'm supposed to help others that struggle with the same issues that I struggle with." I decided I was going to start a men's group with the other men in my DV class. I verified this with my congruency matrix, and it was clearly the right thing to do.

The morning of my first group, I was so excited and filled with energy that I couldn't stand it! I'd invited a number of men from class to join me but only a few showed up. It didn't matter, though. I still shared with them and taught them everything I had learned.

Unfortunately, this group only lasted a few weeks. Before I knew it, the men weren't showing up. Their pain wasn't great enough to drive them to change, so change didn't happen. I later heard that most people who struggle with DV never overcome it, and now I understand why.

I didn't give up though. I kept looking for opportunities to add value to people's lives. Bob and I created a goal setting course from the concepts he taught me and began teaching it to others. We taught it at the Union Gospel Mission in downtown Seattle. We taught it to the leadership team of Prisoners for Christ. I taught it at my church. I was so excited about it that I taught my mom, my dad, my brothers and my sisters. I taught it to people at work. I shared it with my counselors and with my pastors, both current and former.

I was so excited about this new approach that I couldn't sleep at night. I found myself once again getting edgy and irritable. One night at eleven, I was so excited that I called Bob. He should have known something was up, but he didn't say anything. I was showing all the signs of being hypomanic, but I didn't know it. I was high on life and I loved it!

I would later discover that one of the side effects of my antidepressant is that it can trigger episodes of mania in bipolar people, and this is what happened with me. This wouldn't be the first instance of hypomania; it would take me ten more years of trial and error with medication, counseling, exercise, eating, sleeping, and pain to stabilize my moods.

Things at work started to go downhill pretty fast. I found myself yelling in meetings, something I'd never done. I also found myself disagreeing with my bosses' decisions, and instead of following their guidance, I'd do what I thought was right. I was rebelling and not submitting to their guidance. I thought I was smarter than they were and I convinced myself that I didn't have to listen to them.

Something had to change or else I'd be out of a job. Fred, my boss at the time, pulled me into his office and told me that I had to change. He said he cared deeply for me and he wanted to invest in me. He had done some research and discovered a workshop program in San Diego called "The Looking Glass Experience." It was very expensive, but if I was willing to change, the company would pay for it. I told Fred I was willing.

Part of the preparation for the workshop entailed asking my co-workers for feedback, a process known today as "360-degree feedback." I wrote each of them a personal note telling them that I wanted to grow and their feedback was necessary, and that their help was appreciated.

I jumped on a plane to beautiful San Diego for what was going to be one of the most challenging weeks of my career. My personal goals for this session were as follows:

1. Learn how to "tame" my passion by become less overbearing
2. Learn how to be a "people person"
3. Learn how to live a "balanced" life

We split into small groups, each under the guidance of one of the leaders at the Looking Glass Experience. They taught us principles of leadership and they talked about the power of feedback, introducing us to the tool known as the Johari

Window and the concept of using feedback from others to reveal our "blind spots." The program would reveal our blind spots and provide the tools to improve them.

We began a two-day simulation exercise with our small team. I was so excited that I immediately started taking charge and telling everyone what we were going to do and how we were going to do it.

"Whoa," one of them said. "Slow down, you aren't God, and you can't tell us what to do!"

I immediately argued back, "I'm not God, but I do this for a living and I've been recognized as a leader by my company for my skills. I'm going to lead us."

The instructor piped in. "Damon, your company also recognized that you have a problem when working with people. That's why you are here."

That hurt. So much so that I instantly changed my behavior. Begrudgingly, I sat down and listened. We proceeded with the simulation and debriefed at the end of the day.

"There were people observing your behavior behind the two-way glass. You'll hear their feedback on our last day," the instructor shared.

"Awesome," I thought. "They'll tell everyone else that I was right and I'll be justified about my aggressive behavior."

The next day, the evaluators gave us feedback from our work. They presented us with the data from a tool called *SkillScope*. I love data, so I put it into a spreadsheet and summarized the findings: I needed to improve managing conflict, negotiation, building relationships, and being more flexible. My strongest points were energy, drive, ambition, risk taking, and solving problems.

Category	Gap
Managing Conflict; Negotiation	80%
Relationships	68%
Openness To Influence; Flexibility	56%
Getting Information, Making Sense of it; Problem identification	19%
Risk-Taking, Innovation	16%
Energy, Drive, Ambition	8%

This was awesome! I could now take my skills as a Six Sigma Master Black Belt to improve myself! As painful as my areas for improvement were, I couldn't argue with the data. People I respected provided it. People I'd worked with for 8 hours a day, many for the full ten years I'd worked there. Furthermore, the data aligned with the problems I was having in my marriage.

I had a major blind spot and I could no longer ignore it. I went to dinner alone that night, reflecting on the feedback I'd received. I wrestled with what it was telling me, and I started beating myself up again. The old voice crept back into my head "You're a monster; you'll never change."

But I had a stronger voice now. "I am a man of integrity and I care deeply for people. I commit to worthy goals."

Accepting the feedback and taking action to improve it was perfectly congruent with the man I wanted to become. I stopped agonizing over the feedback and accepted it, excited and ready to use it to help me change.

The next day, my team went through the most powerful exercise on feedback that I've ever experienced. The instructor warned us that this exercise would be extremely challenging, but if we were open to what we heard, it could change our lives. He set a tape recorder in the middle of the table and put a blank cassette tape into it. Each of us would have a turn, and we'd follow a process known as "S.B.I.A."

Situation: What was the specific situation that this feedback was related to?

Behavior: What behavior was observed during this situation?

Impact: What impact did this behavior have on those around you?

Action: What action will you take to ensure this behavior is changed?

When it was our turn, each person around the table would provide feedback using the S.B.I.A. model. During the whole week, we were being observed through the two-way glass, and the observers would share their feedback with us. Finally, our instructor said that he would wrap up the recording with his feedback. All participant feedback would be recorded on the cassette tape so that we could listen to it later.

"Who'd like to go first?"

"Sure, I'll do it," I said.

"Okay, Damon. There are only 2 rules, and you must follow them. After each person provides their feedback, you must listen but you can't talk. After the person finishes with the feedback you must look them in the eye and say, 'Thank you for the feedback.'"

And so it began. "Damon, my feedback is based on our first interaction. Situation: We sat down as a team to put a plan together, and you immediately said, 'I have a tool for this, let's use it.' Behavior: When the team resisted using the tool, you kept pushing and pushing to use it and wouldn't stop. You didn't listen to the team and wasted a lot of our time. Impact: The team lost precious time, and you lost your ability to influence us. You were so intent on imposing your will that you steamrolled us. Damon, you act like you're God but you aren't."

I was burning inside to argue that I was right, but every time I tried, the instructor said, "Damon, listen."

I listened and my first teammate provided feedback I looked him in the eye and said, "Thank you for the feedback."

This is just an anomaly, I thought. I can't wait to hear how good I am from the rest of the team! But I didn't get the reactions I expected. The feedback continued to reveal a few very strong patterns in my behavior.

"Damon," another teammate started, "When we were in the simulation and time crunched, there was a lot of pressure on everyone. We all needed to work like a team and trust each other by listening and following through with our assignments. Behavior: Damon, you didn't listen. Instead, you argued your point, insisting you were right and growing more and more angry in the process. I observed your ears turning red and a scowl on your face. Impact: You overpowered your teammates and slowed the whole team down. Eventually, the team learned to not include you in critical decisions."

"Thank you for the feedback."

My third teammate unloaded. "Situation: Damon, I don't have a specific example, but I observed your passion during the entire session. You were always hyper-focused on getting results, and you helped the team get great results. Behavior: You never smiled during the whole activity. You were always tense, and you had no peace during the process. Impact: As a leader, when you exhibit peace the whole team exhibits peace. When you are tense and exhibit this tension, the whole team is tense and becomes stressed very quickly. Your intensity and passion impacted the team's ability to enjoy the process. You need to find internal peace."

"Thank you for the feedback."

My fourth teammate continued. "Situation: Damon, when the team was struggling to make a decision, I observed you striving to bring the whole team to consensus. Behavior: You introduced a simple tool that helped the whole team come to consensus. Impact: The whole team functioned as a team because we'd made a joint decision. Nice job, Damon."

"Thank you for the feedback."

The observers and our instructor shared their feedback, which was similar to what I'd already heard.

"Thank you for the feedback," I said.

The instructor took the tape out of the cassette player, "I'd recommend you listen to this occasionally as a reminder," he said. "You did a great job of listening to the feedback."

Now I'd seen quantified feedback from my peers and supervisors at work, direct feedback from a group of people and facilitators that observed me in a "pressure cooker" situation. I also received the written comments from my peers and supervisors at work.

I summarized my strengths and weaknesses:

Weaknesses	Strengths
"A hard driving, inflexible individual who puts results in the way of relationships. Difficult to negotiate with, and very poor at developing relationships with people. Often times implements solutions and doesn't follow through. Rarely learns from mistakes"	*"A fact-based individual who attacks problems with an incredible passion and zeal. Has the ability to rapidly accumulate information to focus a team on business priorities. Takes risks and rapidly solves problems to get major business results."*

Even though this feedback hurt, it was just what I needed. If I wanted to continue growing in my career, I needed to change. It was now more painful to stay the same than it was to change.

As I sat on the plane flying back to Seattle, I decided that I no longer wanted to be that person. I was going to do whatever it took to change. What I didn't know is that changing would require me to dig deep into my past to expose the pain from my childhood that drove the majority of my behavior.

Questions to Consider

- Do you make decisions based on emotion or principle?
  - Why?
- How do you proactively seek feedback to identify your blind spots?
  - How do you respond when hearing feedback that is painful?
- What is your biggest area in need of improvement?
  - Have you written down your goals to improve in this area?
- How can I help you?
  - You can find more resources and my contact information at **www.paindriveschange.com**.

5
The Pain of the Father Void

And a voice from heaven said, "This is my Son,
whom I love; with him I am well pleased."
—Matthew 3:17 NIV

Steamroller? Puts results ahead of relationships? Difficult to work with? Poor at developing relationships with people?

These words went through my head for days after my seminar week in San Diego. Fortunately, I had a set of Unifying Life Principles to weigh these behaviors against, and it was obvious that these behaviors were not congruent with the man I was striving to be. Something needed to change, and the pain was providing me the motivation to change.

When I returned to work, I took the advice of my counselor and wrote a personal thank-you note to everyone who had provided feedback. I gave them the results of the comments, and I told them that I intended to change my behavior. Furthermore, having experienced the power of feedback in a safe environment, I granted them the freedom to confront me if they ever observed any of these behaviors again.

I had humbled myself enough to ask for their help. Using their feedback, I then put a process in place that would hold me accountable. To resolve this issue, I would use the same Six Sigma continuous improvement process that I'd successfully used so many times before in solving problems on the manufacturing floor at Honeywell.

First, I defined the problem I was trying to solve and the objective.

Problem

My current behaviors at work are severely hindering my ability to grow in my career and are damaging the relationships with my peers. If I don't change my conduct, I could ultimately lose my job and my ability to provide for my family.

Objective

Transform my behaviors at work to be fully congruent with my Unifying Life Principles and always prioritize relationships at work above results.

If I could accomplish this objective, I would grow in my career and enrich my life through deeper meaningful relationships.

Measurement

I would need a way to measure my progress against these goals. This was easy. I'd received quantitative feedback from my peers and also qualitative feedback. My measurement would be through the feedback from my peers and supervisors at work. Did they see an improvement in my behavior?

Analyze Root Cause

I would have to analyze the problem and identify its root cause. Through this process I would identify the origin of many of my behavioral issues.

> *"For every thousand hacking at the leaves of evil,*
> *there is one striking at the root."*
> —Henry David Thoreau

In order to discover the root cause of my behavioral issues I'd need to dig deep into my childhood.

I was the youngest of 5 children from my mom and dad. Danny is my oldest brother, followed by Debbie then Dean (he died in a car accident when I was seventeen), then D'Ann is my next older sister. All of my brothers and sisters were born about a year apart, but I was born 5 years after my sister, D'Ann. Mom tells me that the Electrolux vacuum cleaner salesman was trying to close the deal, but she had to tell him to come back later because I was ready to enter the world!

She didn't make it to Spokane, and on December 4, 1967, I was born in Davenport, Washington. My earliest family memory came when I was only a toddler. It was very cold in our house when I came downstairs that morning for breakfast. Everyone was sitting at the table when Dad said, "Kids, we have something to tell you. We are getting divorced, and I won't be living here anymore."

I was obviously too young to remember many of the details, but the emotional trauma of my dad leaving me and the family when I needed him the most left a huge hole in my heart, my "Father Void." Even though I was the youngest, I must have felt the need to be "the man of the house."

As I mentioned earlier, I remember it being cold in our house—always. I got up that morning to warm it up for everyone. I opened the oven door and put some paper in it after turning the burner on. A fire immediately started. It quickly got out of hand, though, and was on the verge of spreading when, fortunately, my mom rushed in and put the fire out.

It was cold, and Dad wasn't home to keep us warm or to protect us. Even now when I feel cold in my house, I experience deep emotional pain, and that fear of not being warm and protected overwhelms me. God created fathers to protect their families, and he made us with a need for that protection. When that protection is removed through divorce, death, or abandonment by fathers, it wreaks havoc on the lives of the children.

A study in 2010 by the U.S. Census Bureau indicates that 33% of America children live without fathers in their homes. Another study in 2012 by the U.S. Census Bureau indicated that 57.6% of black children, 31.2% of Hispanic children, and 20.7% of white children are living absent their biological fathers. If it were classified as a disease, fatherlessness would be an epidemic worthy of attention as a national emergency.

Here are some key statistics from fathers.com on the impact of fatherlessness:

- 71% of high school dropouts come from fatherless homes
- 70% of pregnant teenagers come from fatherless homes
- 80% of adolescents in psychiatric hospitals come from fatherless homes
- 90% of homeless and runaway children come from fatherless homes
- 63% of youth suicides come from fatherless homes
- 70% of adolescents in juvenile correctional facilities come from fatherless homes
- 71% of adolescent substance abusers come from fatherless homes

Furthermore, children from fatherless homes are:

- 10 times more likely to abuse chemical substances
- 4 times more likely to be raised in poverty
- 11 times more likely to have violent behavior
- 20 times more likely to be incarcerated
- 9 times more likely to drop out of school
- 9 times more likely to be raped or sexually abused

- 2 times as likely to commit suicide

Mom and Dad ended up divorcing. Dad moved to Kettle Falls, a small town about 2 hours from where we lived in Grand Coulee. Even though he wasn't in my home while I was growing up, I still spent time with him. Dad tried hard to see us as much as he could.

I have warm memories of listening to *The Carpenters* on his 8-track tapes while we rode in his little truck from Grand Coulee to Kettle Falls. We spent many summers in Kettle Falls riding my dirt bike, fishing, and swimming in Lake Roosevelt.

But Dad remarried and built a new family of his own. He adopted one son and they had another son. They had a nice stable home and they loved one other. Sometimes I visited after Christmas. It hurt me deeply when I saw all of the presents his new family had. Why didn't I get that many presents, I wondered? Even though he loved me as much as he loved them, as a young boy this made me feel differently.

One day while I was in grade school, I won an award for an essay I'd written. I was so proud of myself that I wanted to share it with my dad. I rushed over to the payphone across the street and dialed 0 for the operator. I didn't have any change, so I asked to place a collect call to my dad. With excitement in my heart, I waited anxiously for his response.

"Damon Stoddard is on the line; will you accept his collect call?" the operator asked.

"No, I won't," was the answer on the other end.

I was crushed, and I couldn't understand why my collect call wasn't accepted. I desperately wanted to share my accomplishment.

I rushed home bawling hysterically, feeling like my dad was abandoning me. Didn't he love me? In this crushing moment, I believe I made a subconscious decision in my heart that I would earn his love and approval. I would do whatever I needed to do, and he would love me just like he loved his new family.

When I got home, Mom asked what had happened. I told her that I'd won an award at school and tried to tell Dad but my call wasn't accepted.

"That's just your dad, Son. He's not being a father to you." Mom was bitter at Dad and spoke poorly of him, something no parent should ever do, no matter how angry. But in that instant, she justified my hurt toward my dad, igniting a flame of anger in my heart toward him that would burn brighter and stronger for the next 25 years of my life.

From this point forward, my relationship with my dad only got worse. As I mentioned earlier, I had to go to a foster home when I was 8. The first foster home didn't work out, so I went to a boy's ranch in Manson, Washington, right before the start of third grade. I lived in this boy's ranch until the beginning of my fifth grade year when my brother and sister, Mom, and I moved back to Grand Coulee.

My foster dad's name was Gene. He had about a dozen boys in the boy's ranch. Gene wasn't married, so he took care of the boys alone. Gene quickly became the father that I needed so deeply. He took me in as his own son and spoiled me. "You're the apple of my eye," he used to tell me. He bought me a motorcycle when I was 9 and took me on special trips with a few other boys across the country to Disneyworld. He showered me with gifts and loved me.

One day I went to the dentist and the dentist recommended that I get a retainer, but that it would be costly. Gene told me he had called my dad, and Dad refused to pay for my retainer. Gene began badmouthing him, saying "If he was a good dad he'd pay for this. I'll pay for it myself." Of course, this only added fuel to the burning anger I already had. And, it gave me one more reason to love Gene more as my foster dad.

Little boys need their dad, and I was particularly vulnerable during this season of my life. My mom was trying to rebuild her life so we could be together, and my dad was rebuilding his life with his new family. Gene capitalized on that vulnerability.

On one of my first nights at his foster home, he came into my bedroom. I was on the top bunk. He talked to me and encouraged me, then he put his hand in my underwear.

That was weird, I thought, and asked him to stop.

But he didn't. He continued fondling my genitals saying, "This is normal, just enjoy it. This is what dads do with their sons."

A little boy of 8 doesn't know right from wrong. Even though I had a sense that what he was doing was wrong, I believed him. Gene knew I was vulnerable and could sense my deep desire to have a father. I was easy prey for him. Gene regularly fondled me, always telling me it was okay, "this is what dads do with their sons," he would say.

Occasionally, he would come into the bathroom while I was showering and fondle me, always justifying his despicable actions by telling me, "It's okay. This is what dads do with their sons." The more time Gene spent with me, the more he knew I was "easy prey," so he continued spoiling me and taking me on trips around the country. One day we drove to the motorcycle shop and he bought me a brand new motorcycle. The more he spoiled me the more attached I became to him. The more attached I became to him the more I saw him as the father that I needed so badly.

When I moved to Grand Coulee, he wrote me letters and

many times drove 2 hours each way to pick me up for the weekends. He bought my mom a car and gave her gas money for driving me back and forth as well, and he paid her to work for him while I was there.

One Christmas, he came down and had what seemed like a carload of presents for me. We were poor so Christmas usually meant 1 or 2 presents. But this Christmas was special!

As I mentioned earlier, I was particularly vulnerable at Christmas, so when Gene showed up with the carload of presents, I was filled with love.

"Dads do this for their boys."

Birthdays were special with Gene at the boy's ranch. We had lots of presents, cake, and special meals. This, too, was a point of vulnerability for me. Dad rarely remembered my birthday, but Gene did!

"Dads do this for their boys," Gene would say.

I was getting older and began to understand that what he was doing wasn't right, so I tried telling him to stop. He didn't stop.

We should have known something was wrong when he packed up everything and moved to Texas. He said that he loved me so much that he invited me down, so I spent much of the summer there with him. I remember how hot it was and how Gene would go to work in the morning and come home in the evening while I stayed at home. I don't remember for sure, but I think I might have been the only boy living with him that summer, at most there were 2 others. Gene, of course, took advantage of this opportunity and continued fondling me regularly.

By summer's end, I went home. Gene told mom to meet him at the Washington State line and he drove me there and dropped me off. Gene gradually stopped contacting me. He was completely out of my life by the time I started seventh grade. My own dad had left me when I was a toddler, and now my "new dad" left me too. In my heart, I felt the words that Gene said so many times: "Dads do this for their boys."

I was sitting in an assembly in our school gym when my teacher told me that I needed to go home. Arriving there, Mom and 2 men were sitting around the kitchen table. They introduced themselves and said, "Damon, we're from the FBI. We're here to ask you some questions about Gene."

They asked me if he had fondled me. I told them that he had, sharing the details of how often he did it. They informed me that other boys had started talking to their parents about what Gene was doing, and one of the parents had contacted the police. The FBI got involved because Gene no longer lived in the same state. Ten to twenty boys had reported that Gene had fondled them.

I'll never forget the look in my mom's eyes and her words after she heard about what Gene had done to me and the other boys. "If I had that pistol he carried around, I'd blow his head off!" she said.

The FBI told us that they didn't know where Gene was, but they were looking for him. And when they found him, he would be sentenced to years in prison.

I don't know if the FBI ever found Gene, and I've been unsuccessful at locating him. While researching for this book I did, however, find a newspaper article about the boy's home from 1978, the same time that I lived there. One line in the article effectively summarizes why as a little boy I allowed him to do what he did to me:

"....(Gene) feels that his main ingredient for success with the boys is being able to earn their trust...."

Gene earned my trust and manipulated me into believing

that what he did to me was okay. He lied. Dads don't do *that* to their boys.

I was now an adolescent boy and Gene was out of my life while my real dad was building his new family. But now more than ever I needed him in my life. I vowed to do whatever it took to win his approval again. If I'm good enough, I thought, Dad would love me.

I was a straight-A student through junior high and high school. I played football and was one of the team captains. I was senior class president, Spanish club president, and was voted homecoming prince my senior year.

My hurt and anger from my father void came out on the football field. My goal was to hit someone hard enough to hurt him and maybe even take him out of the game. My teammates recognized my need to inflict pain and gave me the "Animal Award" as a senior.

During my last football game, the officials ejected me from the game for punching the guy I'd just tackled.

We were poor so I knew the only way I could go to college would be through scholarships. My teachers recognized my good grades, my extracurricular activities, and my awards. They told me that if I applied for scholarships, I'd likely win some, so I applied for every scholarship I could find. I didn't achieve my goal of valedictorian because of a B-plus I'd received in ninth-grade PE. I had straight A's in every other class from my ninth to twelfth grades and ended up graduating third in my class.

My classmates voted me class speaker at graduation. I was certain I'd earned my father's approval through all of these accomplishments and I desperately wanted to earn his love. I called him on the phone and mentioned that I'd be class speaker and invited him to my graduation.

"Dad, I'm excited about graduation. I'm class speaker, third in my class, and I think I'm going to win a bunch of scholarships. Will you please come?"

"I'm sorry, Son. Since your brother Dean died, my relationship with your mom has been extremely tense and I don't want to be around her. I won't be able to make it."

I can't describe the pain I felt when he said those words. I burst out in tears crying hysterically.

"Dad, I've worked my whole life for your approval and you can't even make it to my graduation?" My tears turned to anger and I started berating him for being such a terrible father, telling him about all of the things he'd done in my life and how badly they hurt me.

Something I said changed Dad's mind. "I'm sorry, Damon. I didn't mean it that way. I'll come, but only for a short while."

Dad came to my graduation and helped me celebrate one of the greatest accomplishments of my life. But his initial response that he couldn't make it hurt me deeply, and I still felt like my efforts to win his approval through my accomplishments failed. In my hurt and anger, I stopped trying to have a relationship. I was now an adult, and I convinced myself that I didn't need him.

One time he told me that he was going to be in Spokane on my birthday and asked if I'd like to have lunch. Wow, I thought. Dad remembered my birthday! We met at McDonalds and I ordered my food expecting him to pay for it, but he didn't.

Dad regretted occasionally forgetting my birthday when I was a boy and was trying hard to make it right, but it backfired on him. He didn't try to hurt me by not paying for my lunch, it was an innocent mistake. But his innocent mistake invoked the hurt in me from all those years as a child when my birthday was forgotten. In a fit of rage, I yelled profanities at him and belittled him. We finished our lunch and went our separate ways.

We visited each other a few times during my twenties making multiple attempts at rebuilding our relationship. When Monica was born I invited him to stay at our house. It was cold outside and we wanted to build a fire in our fireplace. We went outside and I said, "Dad, I don't know how to chop wood. Will you show me?"

"Sure," Dad said, and he showed me how to chop wood.

This is what dads do, I thought to myself.

Dad continued pursuing a relationship with me by calling occasionally, always sending birthday cards, and visiting when he was in Seattle. His continued efforts built a bridge of emotional safety that I would walk across only a few years later.

When I separated from my wife, I learned that Dad had separated from his wife as well. I had a deep need for him and his love during this time. I found a book that described the impact that fathers have on their children when they are absent the home. The book emphasized the importance of reconciling with your father if he was absent, and it talked about the profound impact forgiveness would have on both the father and the child.

After all he'd done to me, I could never forgive him, I thought. But the pain of being without him was greater than the pain of trying to reconcile our relationship. I began talking to my counselor about my desire to heal my father wound. He recommended that I call my dad and invite him over to have a joint counseling session.

I nervously dialed his number and began sharing some of

what I was learning about the importance of fathers. I shared how I was angry with him and told him that I didn't want to live my life with the anger.

I asked him the question, "Dad, would you be willing to come over and attend a joint counseling session with me?"

"Yes, Son. That would be great. I want to reconcile our relationship."

I was elated, and we set a date. On the days leading up to our counseling appointment, I was nervous and scared. "Would my dad abandon me again?" I asked myself.

But he didn't.

April 17, 1999, was the most incredible day of my life. Dad arrived and we drove to the counseling session together.

Larry, my counselor, asked us to state what our goals were for the session, and we both shared that we wanted to heal our relationship. Larry commended my dad's courage and decision, noting that in his career as a counselor, he'd only had a handful of dads willing to work it out with their sons.

Larry then told us that it would be very intense emotionally, but to keep us civil, there were a few rules to observe. "First, when one of you talks," he said, "just listen. Do not interrupt, do not express your anger—just listen."

We both agreed.

I went first. "For my whole life I've tried to win your approval but I feel like I've failed. I desperately needed a dad during so many years of my life." I told Dad about how angry I was with him. In great detail I recalled to him the times that hurt the most.

Dad listened quietly as I spoke. He didn't try to justify his behavior; he didn't get angry—he just listened.

I finally finished my recitation. Dad looked me in the eye

and asked me 4 words that would change my life and the lives of my bloodline for generations.

"Will you forgive me?"

Tearfully, I said, "Yes, Dad, I forgive you."

We hugged and Larry said, "Okay, now it's your turn to share your story, Ray."

Dad began telling me about his life, about how he didn't have a relationship with his dad and how he ultimately decided to move away from home at a very young age. He always dreamed of a family, the family he didn't have growing up. He shared how he met my mom and about their decision to get married. Their marriage was very rough, and he described some of the things that happened between them that damaged their relationship.

He then paused and said, "I want you to know I don't blame your mom for our failed marriage. I take responsibility for my own actions."

Eventually the pain of being married was greater than the pain of divorce and so they decided to get a divorce.

He shared how he desperately tried to keep the family together and see everyone regularly, but that ultimately he couldn't do it with a family of 5 kids, so he began isolating to deal with his own pain. He deeply regretted not being there for us kids growing up, and he didn't think he could ever forgive himself for it.

Dad said he tried desperately to have a relationship with me as an adult, but I wouldn't let him in. It hurt him that I wouldn't let him in, but he vowed he would never stop trying to form a relationship.

Finally, he shared how much it meant to him that I took the initiative to arrange this counseling session.

With tears in my eyes, I looked at Dad and said, "Dad,

will you forgive me?"

"Yes, Son, I forgive you."

We hugged each other tightly. Those 4 simple words, "Will you forgive me?" wiped away thirty-one years of pain. They changed the destiny of my children, and their children, and their children, and...

Those 4 simple words would finally end the generational curses that had plagued our families for generations.

...I lay the sins of the parents upon their children; the entire family is affected—even children in the third and fourth generations of those who reject me.
—Exodus 20:5

Larry commended us and congratulated us. He told us it wouldn't be easy but that we could make up for the lost years and have a stronger relationship because of it. He told us to talk to each other regularly on the phone and to always say "I love you" after we were done. He said it would be awkward, but to keep doing it.

Dad and I spent the weekend together. I pulled out the camcorder to capture the emotions we were both feeling.

"I want to share with you the most incredible day of my life...." I said and I proceeded to share the details of what I've written here.

"I do want to say this has been a great weekend and one of the best things that has happened to me," Dad said, and he proceeded to share the details of what I've written here.

The day before, Dad had shared this picture with me, it was the first time I'd ever seen it. This was one of the last pictures taken before they were divorced. He shared that he always wanted a family and dreamed about it, but it just didn't work.

When I saw the picture and heard his words, my heart was filled with deep compassion for him. In that instant, I realized that my dad had the same dream for his life that I'd written down just a month earlier. A dream of family and love. And I realized that Dad couldn't go back in time and have that dream. His dream had died and I felt the deep pain he had for what he'd done.

I cried and cried and cried. All of the hurt and anger that I'd felt my whole life came out through my tears and was replaced with compassion and love. That compassion and love has grown over the years, and today, I have an incredible relationship with my dad. We talk on the phone every week and see each other a few times a year, always telling each other "I love you" as we are leaving. One year, my step mom told me that Dad would really like me to visit him at his home. That would be inconvenient, I thought, he lives 5 hours away and his house is small, my family wouldn't be comfortable. But then I remembered one of my unifying life principles: "Honor my mother and father." I visited Dad and we had a great time.

Nearly every summer, we make that 5-hour drive as a family and camp in Dad's backyard for a few days. We sit in his backyard under his shade tree and listen to *The Carpenters* while he plays with his grandkids. We are a family, and my children love their grandpa. He always remembers birthdays and sends gifts at Christmas. Together, we are enjoying the dream that we thought was lost so many years ago.

I asked Dad to share a little bit from his perspective in hopes that it will help you find the courage in your pain to be the father you want to be.

Dad's Letter

I wanted to have a family. It was my dream, too.

After I was married for a few years I was working at a sawmill that got its logs from floating them behind a large boat. I began working on the boat but it called for being away from home for a week or 2 at a time. *Bad things kept happening in our marriage and I was at a loss and didn't know what to do.* Being away only made things worse and eventually things got so bad that I asked for a divorce.

Your mom moved away with you children. I was in so much pain that I couldn't stand it anymore. After all of the stuff that happened when I was married to your mom my dream was gone, and when I had the opportunity to start all over I took it. I remarried and had 2 boys. I couldn't seem to find the time to go and visit you kids very often.

I know I did a lot of things wrong and I am not proud of myself. There were reasons for it but I didn't have the courage to keep fighting it. I missed you kids deeply, but I rarely heard from any of you. I never received letters or phone calls from anyone (except you) to share your lives with me. I never knew how any of you were doing in school or who your friends were.

So all I'm saying is I was hurting bad during that time period. You all were hurting, but it didn't have to happen. We could have been a happy family. All I wanted was to have a family like you have now and I am sorry.

When you became an adult I continued pursuing a relationship with you even though you pushed me away time after time. When you called and asked me to join you for counseling I was very nervous. I'd been hurt by you so many times before and I expected to be hurt again. I was so happy that we had the conversation during that counseling session. It was one of the best days of my life and it changed our relationship forever. Who knows where we'd both be today if we hadn't forgiven each other during that counseling session!

I am thankful for our relationship today and I am grateful for the relationship I have with my grandchildren!

I love you all and I wish it could have been different.

—Dad

I love you Dad, and today I can truly empathize with what you must have gone through. I forgive you. I love and respect you today more than I ever have because of how you responded when I repeatedly treated you so poorly. You pursued me when I pushed you away. Your courageous decision to attend counseling with me that day years ago changed the lives of generations.

Questions to Consider

- How's your relationship with your dad?
  - What do you need to do to make it better?
- How's your relationship with your kids?
  - What do you need to do to make it better?
- How can I help you?
  - You can find more resources and my contact information at **www.paindriveschange.com**.

6
The Joy of Being Re-Parented

*Dear children, let us not love with words or
speech but with actions and in truth.*
—1 John 3:18

Yesterday was a very hard but rewarding day. I had just finished writing the chapter on "The Pain of the Father Void," and it brought up many painful memories.

I decided that my writing would honor my parents. However, I feel strongly that the power of our story comes through an understanding of the bad times, so I should write about the bad times as well.

I called Dad and told him that I'd just written the chapter, but it might be painful for him to read. Because I didn't want it to hurt him, I repeatedly reminded him that there was a reason for everything that happened and that I wouldn't be the man I am today if we hadn't gone through years of turmoil. Furthermore, I promised him we wouldn't publish anything unless we both approved it.

My respect for my dad grew enormously yesterday. He told me that he didn't want to hash through those memories, but if our story could help other people he was all for it. We talked on the phone last night after he'd read it. He said, "I'm okay with it, Damon, you can publish it."

"The day we went to counseling changed my life forever. I'm so thankful for our relationship. We can't change history, but we can change the future," he said.

He then proceeded to share his heart with me about how some of my actions still hurt him. It hurt me to hear him describe his feelings that sometimes my actions cause him pain. But that's what dads do—they speak the truth in love to their children because they want what's best for them. Even though now I'm 47, I still need to hear those words of truth from my dad so that my actions will be congruent with the man I want to be.

I thanked Dad for his honesty and told him I would work hard to change my actions because my heart's desire was to honor him.

"I'm proud of you son. I love you."

Dads, you may not realize how much power your words have on your children. You might be hesitant to discipline them when they need to be disciplined. Your children need your discipline, but it will only be effective if it comes from your heart—and they know it. Dad's discipline of me last night was heartfelt, and it will effectively change my behavior.

After we hung up, I went downstairs with a strong sense of peace. Our conversation was one of the deepest and most heartfelt that we had ever shared, and I needed disciplining for my behavior. Thanks, Dad!

All discipline for the moment seems not to be joyful,
but sorrowful; yet to those who have been trained by it,
afterwards it yields the peaceful fruit of righteousness.
Therefore, strengthen the hands that are weak and the knees
that are feeble, and make straight paths for your feet,
so that the limb which is lame may not be put out of joint,
but rather be healed.
—Hebrews 12:11-13

Years earlier in my video diary I shared how Dad had disciplined me a couple of times right after our counseling session and how much I appreciated it. I don't remember ever being disciplined by either Mom or Dad while I was growing up; they didn't discipline me when I made mistakes. Like all sons, I needed to be disciplined.

Parents are the first authority figure in a child's life. Children learn how to respond to authority based on how they respond to their parents' authority. By not being disciplined, I learned that I was the ultimate authority and that I could do anything I wanted. I made the rules, so essentially, I was my own God. When rules were imposed on me or something happened that displeased me, I would resort to power and, at times, violence, to get my own way. Like a naughty child, I would kick, scream, and throw a fit until I got my way.

For me to be the man God wanted me to be, I had to grow up.

When I moved into the little red house in South Seattle, I knew it would only be temporary. The house was for sale, and we didn't have a plan for where I'd live after it sold.

I had lived there for only a few months when it sold. A few weeks were all I had before the house closed and I'd have to move out, so I had to quickly find a place to live. I couldn't move back into my home because there was a protection order against me. Besides, my wife and I weren't healthy enough to live together.

I went to work and I told Steve that I didn't know what to do. We had spent a lot of time together, and he was very aware of my situation.

"Damon, I have an unfinished room in my garage, but it's livable. Why don't you come stay there and live with us for a few months?"

"Really? That would be great!"

Before I knew it, I was living in a small room that was

under construction deep in the woods of Issaquah. Steve and Sue didn't have a TV, which was very odd to me. I'd grown up with a TV and I used it as a way to escape my pain. Fortunately, I had my TV and laser disc player. Laser discs were before DVDs and were twelve inches in diameter. I had quite a collection of movies on laser disc, so I figured I'd hook my TV and laser disc up and watch movies in my new room.

Steve had warned me that the room wasn't finished, but I didn't care. It had a bed and I had my TV. I plugged my laser disc into the nearest outlet. All of a sudden I heard a crackling sound and I saw smoke coming from my laser disc player. I quickly unplugged it and called Steve out to figure out what happened.

Steve chuckled and said, "Oh, I'm sorry. I forgot to tell you—that outlet is wired for 220 volts. It must have fried the circuit board. I'm pretty handy; we'll tear it apart and see if we can fix it."

Steve was very handy and I'm sure he could have fixed it, but he never did. He knew I didn't need TV at this time. What I really needed was family, and I needed God.

A few hours after moving into his guesthouse, Steve began parenting me. Over the next 3 months, Steve and his wife, Sue, took me into their home as one of their children. They loved me, cared for me, disciplined me, and supported me.

On the first evening, Sue said, "We're having dinner at 6, will you be joining us?" I love food, especially when I don't have to cook it, so I jumped at the opportunity.

The whole family gathered at the table and bowed their heads. Steve prayed over our meal, thanking God for His provision.

We enjoyed dinner together and they invited me to stay

with them and hang out.

Looking around, I didn't see a TV. I thought to myself, "ummm...what will we do? There isn't a TV to watch."

I didn't have anything else to do, so I stayed with them. We talked and talked and talked. I would ask them questions about my situation, looking for guidance. Steve would always pull out his Bible, and we would start searching for God's wisdom. In this way, Steve trained me to go to my Bible for answers.

Years earlier, right after I gave my heart to the Lord, I went into Steve's office and shut the door. "Steve, I have great news! I've given my heart to the Lord!" I exclaimed.

"Praise God," Steve said, "We've been praying for you since the day I interviewed you and we hired you at Sundstrand." He pulled a Bible off his shelf, signed it, and he encouraged me to go to it whenever I needed wisdom.

Now, years later, he was modeling how he always consulted the Bible. Wisdom is more caught than taught. Spending time with Steve and Sue, I caught their wisdom.

They loved Monica dearly. She was barely eighteen months old. Easter was coming and I had Monica that weekend. Sue asked me what I was going to do for Monica on Easter morning. I was clueless, and she knew it.

"Sue, I don't know what to do," I said.

"That's okay, Damon. I hope you don't mind but I bought Monica a few things for Easter morning."

She pulled out a basket and a small stuffed bunny. "Do you think Monica will like this?"

"Absolutely!" I said, excitedly.

That Easter morning, Monica woke up to find a basket and a stuffed bunny. She grabbed the bunny and held it tightly. We then opened the basket to discover candy and some bubbles to play with. I blew bubbles with her while she held her new bunny close to her chest.

"What will we call your new bunny?" I asked Monica. As I thought of the bubbles we'd been blowing, I asked, "How about Bubbles?"

Monica turned eighteen a few days ago. Bubbles has been with Monica through the good times as well as the bad times. When her mom moved away, Bubbles was with Monica. When Monica struggled with friendships at school, Bubbles was with her. When I remarried, Bubbles was with her. On our wedding day, I performed a little ceremony with Teddy, her stepsister Amanda's stuffed bear, and they were married, too.

When Monica struggled with addiction and went away to a treatment center, Bubbles was with her. I bet Bubbles will be with Monica when she marries, and I wager that Monica's daughter will have Bubbles as her best friend, too.

Sue knew what Monica needed and gave it to her when I didn't have the wisdom to do so.

Once, when Monica was doing something I didn't allow, I yelled, "Stop!" But she didn't stop; she kept doing what she was doing. "Monica, I said stop!" I yelled again. But once again, she didn't stop. I went over to her and pulled her away.

"Monica, when Daddy says *stop*, you need to stop."

Steve and Sue watched but didn't say a word. Later that evening, I put Monica to bed and came back into the house for some evening conversation.

"Damon, may we share some observations with you?" they asked.

"Umm…sure," I hesitantly said, as I was overwhelmed with a deep sense of fear that I was going to be yelled at myself.

"Damon, Monica needs to trust her daddy. When you tell her to do something more than once, you are training her to not trust you. If you want Monica to trust you, then you'll need to change how you discipline her," Steve said.

"One of your most important jobs as a father is to earn Monica's trust. When she trusts you, she will listen to you. When she gets older, this trust will allow you to speak into her heart, and she'll come to you when she needs help."

"Monica will relate to God like she relates to you. If she learns to trust you, her earthly father she can see, then she will learn to trust God, whom she can't see."

"Damon, tell her only once. If she doesn't respond, you'll have to increase the pain until it's more painful for her to stay the same than it is to change her behavior. This might mean spanking her."

"Damon, when you discipline her, you must never do it in anger. Only discipline in love or she won't respond and will begin rebelling. You want to produce the righteousness of God in her, and the Bible says that the anger of man does not produce the righteousness of God."

"If you spank her, you must ensure that you've reached her heart. Pray with her afterwards, and teach her to ask Jesus to forgive her sin."

"After you're done, teach her to ask forgiveness of you. Then and only then, you should hug her and hold her, telling her she is forgiven and that you love her. If you do this correctly, you will only have to spank her a few times."

"OK," I said. "I'll do it."

A few days later, I had an opportunity to test what I'd learned. Monica was acting up, and I looked at her sternly and said, "Stop."

She didn't stop.

I walked over to her, looked her in the eye, and told her I'd have to discipline her because I loved her. I told her to put her nose in the corner.

A few minutes later, I told her to come sit on my lap. She wanted to hug me but I told her not yet. I prayed with her, and we asked Jesus for forgiveness. Afterwards, I told her she needed to ask me for forgiveness as well. She did. I then looked her in the eye and told her I loved her and she was forgiven. Then she reached for me and gave me the biggest hug I could remember.

I realized in that moment that Monica had a deep need for my approval. When she did something that I didn't approve of, she knew it. If I didn't correct it immediately, it would cause a separation of her from her father because knowing she'd done something wrong, she would begin hiding from me.

However, when I chose to correct it, she would know I was disappointed. Her need for my approval would be so strong in her heart that it would change her behavior in the future. That's why I needed to wait for her to ask forgiveness, because forgiveness would mean she had owned her behavior in her heart. My hug and affection would assure her that I loved her and wanted only what was best for her.

After I disciplined her that day, Monica was different for the rest of the day. She was relaxed and peaceful, the peaceful fruit of righteousness the Bible promises in Hebrews 12:11.

I shared this experience with Steve and Sue, and they both smiled, seeing that I, too, was experiencing the peaceful fruit of righteousness the Bible promises.

"Damon, do you know why we sin?" Steve asked.

"No, I don't, Steve."

"It all goes back to the garden of Eden. Grab your Bible; let's read Genesis."

We read through the first 3 chapters of Genesis, and Steve shared that our sin began with Adam choosing to disobey God. He pointed out that Adam and Eve knew they'd sinned, and their first response was to hide from God because they were ashamed. When God confronted them, instead of owning up to his disobedience, Adam blamed Eve.

"It's the same way with us," Steve explained. "When we sin, we hide from God. When our children sin, they hide from us. We have to confront sin in our children when we see it, and we need to discipline them until they take full responsibility for their actions and don't blame others. And we need to always remind them that Jesus died on the cross to forgive us of these sins."

Once again, Steve was modeling how to use the Bible to find the answers we need in life.

One day I was doing something that I knew I shouldn't be doing, but I didn't stop. Steve saw this and said, "Damon, come here. I'm going to have to take you out to the woodshed and discipline you."

"What do you mean, Steve?" I asked.

"Damon, when my kids were disobedient and I had to spank them I took them to the woodshed to do it. In our family, 'going to the woodshed' is a metaphor for being disciplined."

Once again, that fear crept up inside of me. What had I done to lose his approval? I dreaded my discipline.

In love, he explained what I'd done. I asked for forgiveness, and he told me I was forgiven.

Afterward, I told Steve I was sorry for my actions, and he told me it was all right. Later that day, I told him once again

"Steve, I'm really sorry for what I did."

"Damon, I've noticed that when you make a mistake you say you are sorry multiple times. If you have to say you're sorry more than once, you're teaching me that I can't trust that you are really sorry."

Hey, I've heard this before I thought!

"Damon, if you strive to be a man of integrity, it will show from your words and your actions. Before you speak a word, make sure that you are willing to stand behind your word. If you can't stand behind your word, don't say it. I think you want to be a man of integrity."

Steve's words penetrated my soul, and I thought about my number one unifying life principle—that of being a man of integrity. His words of wisdom had shown me how to put my desire into action. Before saying, "sorry," I should be sure that I was really sorry. Before telling Monica to stop doing something, I should make sure I meant it. Before committing to something, I should be certain that I would follow through.

A few years ago, Monica asked me if she could go to a concert with a friend and be out past curfew. She really wanted to go to this concert, but I knew she shouldn't go because she had school the next day. So, I told her "No."

"Grrrrrr," she grumbled under her breath, "I guess I shouldn't ask again because you always follow through on your words and never change your mind."

"I love you, Monica," I replied, remembering that conversation with Steve years earlier. He was right.

Steve brought me to the "woodshed" a couple of times in those 3 months, and every time he would discipline me in the same way. Never in anger, always in love, and always forgiving me after my repentance.

When I discipline my own children, I try to do it as Steve taught me.

Every morning when I got up, Sue would have a cup of coffee waiting for me and ask me what I wanted for lunch. She'd pack my lunch as I sat at the kitchen table drinking my coffee. We'd talk and talk and talk. I used to dread getting up in the morning, but with Sue I looked forward to getting up and spending time with her.

I don't drink coffee anymore, but I do enjoy getting up before the kids and spending time just talking and praying with my sweet wife while she makes my lunch.

Steve and Sue lived nearly 25 miles from my house. The protection order was still in force, so I wasn't allowed to transport Monica or pick her up. Steve or Sue always took care of that for me, and they never complained.

One evening, they drove Monica home, but her mom wasn't there. They waited for a while, but she didn't show up. This put them in a very difficult situation. The protection order specified when Monica was to be home, and they had taken her there on time. It was late and Monica needed to be in bed, but by bringing her back to me, they would be violating the court order.

They made a tough decision. They brought Monica back to their house to me.

"Steve, I can go to jail if she calls the police!"

"I know, Damon, but she wasn't there. You won't be responsible for this. If anyone needs to go to jail, I'll go to jail because I made the decision."

Steve held true to his word, and we contacted the courthouse the next day, telling them the situation and asking what he should do to protect me, since it was his decision. They told him to simply write an affidavit and it would be acceptable.

Steve wrote the affidavit.

Steve protected me, modeling for me what parents do for their children. Today, I take my role as the protector of my family very seriously.

Later that evening, Monica's mom called asking Steve to bring Monica back over, saying she had been only a few minutes late, and it was their responsibility to get Monica to her.

Steve said, "Hold on," and looked at me. He told me, "What I'm about to do is going to cause a lot of chaos and she isn't going to like it, but with your permission I'm going to proceed."

I gave him my permission, and he told her that he wouldn't be transporting Monica across the bridge, that she'd have to come pick her up the next morning near his house.

He was right, it caused a lot of chaos. She threatened to call the police, she yelled, she called him names, but Steve wouldn't budge. The next morning she drove the 25 miles to pick Monica up. From this point forward she was always more cooperative and showed much more respect to both Steve and Sue.

Later that morning I asked Steve why he'd chosen to set these firm boundaries. Steve shared that he'd observed a pattern in her behavior that, if not changed, would destroy my ability to have a marriage with her that was based on mutual trust and respect. He shared that he needed me to see how to set boundaries in a loving but firm way so that I could begin setting boundaries that he observed needed to be made in my marriage.

I had never seen or done anything like this. Instead of setting firm boundaries and holding to them, I would set boundaries, but when things got tough, I would back down.

As a result, my relationships weren't based on trust and mutual respect—and they weren't healthy.

From that day forward, I practiced setting firmer boundaries, and I noticed that after I'd set boundaries for the right reasons, I'd feel better about myself. Not only that, but I'd also earn the respect of those I set the boundaries with.

This lesson on boundaries stuck with me. Steve had modeled this behavior to me, so I knew it worked. In the coming years, I would set boundaries that required every bit of courage that I had.

I would have to set boundaries in my marriage and I'd have to set boundaries with Monica when she struggled with addiction as a teen. These boundaries were all necessary, and I believe they may have saved her life. I'll talk more about these decisions later, but through setting these limits, I showed that I could be trusted.

June was rapidly approaching and Steve informed me that he'd be "kicking me out of the nest."

I didn't know where I was going to live, so I asked Steve if I could stay just a little longer.

"I'm sorry, Damon, but it is time for you to spread your wings and fly."

I was shocked and anxious about my finances. "I have only 4 dollars to live on after expenses," I sputtered. "Not only that, but I can't afford to get my own place and I can't move back in with my wife," I begged.

Steve looked closer and said, "Damon, there's something missing from your budget."

"What's that, Steve?"

"I don't see your tithe in the budget, Damon. The Bible says to give the first ten percent of your income as a tithe."

That's crazy, I thought. If I had only dollars to live on, how could I tithe ten percent, and how could I live?

"You need to learn to trust God with your money. You don't have to start by tithing the full ten percent. Start small and be consistent. Slowly start giving more, and God will bless you. Trust Him; He will provide for you."

I took Steve's advice and started tithing, and God did provide. With the selling of my house, I had enough cash to live on for a while.

I counseled with Steve and Bob about where I should live. Should I rent an apartment or a house? Bob offered a solution I never would have thought of.

"Damon, I have a friend who is selling his motorhome. Why don't you buy it and live in it for a while? You can park it in my back yard and live there while you and your wife work things out. You can use the motorhome and go camping with us when we take our motorhome. When you and your wife reconcile, you can camp with her and your family," he said.

A few weeks later, I purchased a motorhome, packed my things, and moved to Bob's backyard. I decided not to pack the laser disc player. I didn't have room in my motorhome for it anyway!

Questions to Consider

- How were you disciplined as a child?
  - Do you discipline your kids the same way?
- Do you need to establish any boundaries in your life?
  - What are they?
- When you apologize, how many times do you say you're sorry?
  - Do you agree with Steve's advice?
- How can I help you?
  - You can find more resources and my contact information at **www.paindriveschange.com**.

7
The Pain of Divorce

*"For I hate divorce," says the Lord, the God of Israel. "And I
hate the man who does wrong to his wife," says the Lord of All.
"So be careful in your spirit, and be one who can be trusted."*
—Malachi 2:16

Hate is a powerful word, especially when it comes from
God. If you're reading this and have either been
divorced or had parents that divorced, I'll bet you hate
divorce, too. When children are involved, they become the
helpless victims of their parents' inability to work things out.

I, too, hated divorce. I watched as divorce wreaked
havoc on the lives of each of my older siblings. I watched
my mom as she divorced 3 times; consequently, I personally
experienced the pain of my parents being divorced. Truth be
told, the divorce rate for my parents and their children is one
hundred percent—more than twice as high as the divorce
rate in America (between forty and fifty percent, depending
on which study you look at).

I detested divorce, and I made a vow to myself that I
wouldn't divorce. Even though the odds were stacked against
me, I would be different. Maybe that's why I didn't have a
girlfriend or even a first kiss until I was seventeen.

That changed when I went to college, though. Like most
teenage boys, I dated many girls until I met my first "real"
girlfriend. Our relationship was good for the first few months,
but then summer break came and I had a job back home in
Grand Coulee. She lived in Spokane and we had to date long

distance, but it didn't work very well.

She and another boy became "friends," and I became very jealous. Our weekend visits quickly degraded into arguments. We went out dancing one evening, and started arguing until I got too angry. I left her to go cool off in the car, but she stayed in the dance hall.

As I sat sulking in the car, I became angrier and angrier until I couldn't stand it any longer. I rushed into the bar. She was talking with another man at the bar. Furious, I walked up behind him and yanked his chair out from under him.

He didn't like that at all. He got up and punched me hard enough to open a gash above my left eye. I was too stubborn to go the emergency room for stitches, so I still have a scar today to remind me of my folly.

When I wasn't with her, I found myself thinking about her constantly. I had a gaping hole in my heart because of the massive trauma I'd experienced as a child. When I was with her and things would go well, that hole would be temporarily filled until we had an argument.

I discovered that how I felt about myself was dependent on how she treated me. When she treated me well, I'd feel great, but when she treated me poorly, that gaping hole would reveal itself and I'd feel terrible. I found myself trying to win her approval, just as I'd tried to earn my dad's approval so many times before.

Eventually, things got worse. We decided to attend a formal dance our college was holding. I was upset that day and began drinking heavily in our motel room with our friends. By the time we left for the dance, I'd had way too much to drink.

My girlfriend loved to dance and started dancing with another man. When I saw her dancing with him, I exploded with anger. I yelled at her to come sit with me. She refused. I kept insisting. My shouts got louder and louder until someone asked the guards to get me out of there.

A couple of burly guys tried to settle me down, but I refused to calm down. I was so out of control that they had to call the police, and I would up spending my first night ever in jail.

A friend of mine and I were roommates, so I called him and asked him to come and bail me out. My girlfriend decided that we should separate for a while to get some healthy space between us.

We separated but I couldn't handle the pain of being abandoned again, like I had been so many times as a child. The pain of abandonment consumed me. I wrote to her, promising that I would change. Eventually, I convinced her to take me back.

Of course, I didn't change, and our pattern of breaking up and getting back together continued for 6 months, until she finally decided to end it completely.

It was the start of my junior year, and I had to transfer to another college to finish my engineering degree. However, going to a different college would mean leaving her. The pain of leaving was greater than the pain of staying, so I chose to stay in hopes that we would get back together.

I took a few classes and began to regain my self-esteem. I'd see her occasionally, but the sight of her re-opened a wound that wasn't going to heal.

I wasn't a Christian at the time, but I did pray when I needed something. Once I asked God to take the pain away and give her back to me. As I was trying to decide where to finish my engineering degree, I sensed that God was prompting me to move to Seattle and complete my schooling there. I didn't know how I was going pay for college, but I did know that if I moved to Seattle, maybe I could find an internship that would pay my college expenses.

I decided to move to Seattle. I wouldn't have to worry about seeing my girlfriend there and could focus on moving forward with my degree and career. When I told her about my decision, she began to cry. She said she missed me and wanted us to date each other again. The thought of losing me for good was too much for her, and she wanted me back.

Nearly overwhelmed with joy, we began dating again. A short while later I moved to Seattle, believing we could make a long distance relationship work by visiting each other on weekends.

But we couldn't. One weekend, I came early to surprise her. She was in the cafeteria sitting with another man. When she saw me, she was very excited. "He was just a friend," she said. But my pain overwhelmed me as I felt like she was betraying me again.

Another big argument ensued. She was fed up and told me, "I'm done with you for good."

I drove back to Seattle while bawling my eyes out. I tried to call her, but she wouldn't talk. I wrote her letters but she wouldn't respond. My first love had abandoned me, invoking the pain of abandonment that I'd felt so often as a child.

Weeks and months went by, and my pain slowly faded away. Then someone told me that she was getting married. It turns out that the man she married was the man she was with that day in the cafeteria! My hope of ever reconciling our relationship was lost.

I lived in a city of millions of people but I felt all alone, so I sought female companionship to replace the loneliness. Each new relationship would temporarily fill the void in my heart, and I would always become dependent on them for my happiness. They would break up with me and I'd be left with the same pain of abandonment that was now characterizing my adult relationships.

When I was twenty-eight, I went home to Grand Coulee for their annual Colorama celebration. It was a beautiful spring day, and I was feeling pretty good. While strolling around at the celebration, I saw a woman that I had grown up with. She was even more beautiful that I had remembered. We chatted for a bit and exchanged phone numbers, both of us feeling like it would be great to see each other again.

I'd just bought a boat and came back to Grand Coulee a few weeks later to go camping, but needed to buy a few items at a flea market for the trip. To my surprise, I ran into her again.

On a whim, I said, "Hey, I'm going camping. Would you like to come along?"

"Sure," she said. "That would be a lot of fun!"

I told her I'd meet her at the boat launch in a few hours and asked her to pack her own food. A few hours later, I picked her up in my boat. She brought her younger daughter, 8, while her older daughter, ten, spent the weekend with friends.

We had a great weekend together, and so began our new relationship.

Life was good! I now had a girlfriend in Grand Coulee, a boat, and it was summertime. I worked during the week in Seattle and spent the evenings with my other girlfriend. On weekends I'd drive to sunny Eastern Washington to be with my new girlfriend! I was never alone and now had 2 women who really liked me!

Unfortunately, it didn't take very long for her to discover

that I had another girlfriend in Seattle. She didn't like this and told me she was breaking up with me. Once again, that fear of abandonment overwhelmed me. I begged her to not to leave me, promising her I'd break up with the girl in Seattle.

My begging worked! We continued dating, but within a few months, the euphoria of a new relationship with weekend fun in the sun was overwhelmed with bickering. Our arguments became more and more heated.

One evening we went to Seattle. My office was having a big party there in the Space Needle restaurant. Unfortunately, we got into a huge argument. On the drive home I snapped and hit her. This was my first episode of DV—but it wouldn't be the last.

When we got home, I quickly apologized and repeatedly told her how sorry I was and that it wouldn't happen again. Irrationally, she believed me and stayed with me that weekend.

She attended church in Grand Coulee and asked me to start joining her. We began attending church on Sundays with her 2 daughters. We were becoming a family, the family we all longed for. I loved those little girls, and they needed a daddy. Their love for me filled my heart and I felt complete when we were together.

When I decided to build a mother-in-law apartment at my house to earn some extra cash, she let me know how she felt about it. She threatened me—if I rented it to a female, she'd break up with me. However, I wasn't going to let her tell me what to do. Defiantly, I ignored her threats and rented the apartment to a woman.

When she found out what I had done, she was furious! I'd never witnessed a woman as angry as she was that evening. She told me we were through. I cried and begged and pleaded with her to not break up with me, but she wouldn't listen.

"We're done, Damon! Goodbye." Click.

Immediately, those all too familiar feelings of abandonment flooded my soul. But this time, the emotions were more intense than I'd ever experienced. Not only was she abandoning me, but her beautiful, young girls were leaving me as well. By breaking up with me, she shattered the dream of having a family I'd held so deeply in my heart for my whole life.

This couldn't happen. I called her repeatedly on the phone but she wouldn't answer. With each failed attempt, the pain intensified. That evening I finally fell asleep but awoke early the next morning to call her. Once again, there was no answer.

I couldn't stand it anymore. I had to escape the pain! I drove to the church we'd been attending in Seattle; and fortunately, the pastor was there. I asked him if we could talk.

I shared how much I loved her and the girls. I told him the pain of our separation was unbearable.

He asked me if I had accepted Jesus as my savior, and I told him I wasn't sure. He asked me if I'd like to accept Jesus as my Lord and Savior right there.

Things looked bleak. She wasn't answering my calls and I needed some relief from my pain, so I decided to make a deal with God. In my mind, I told God that I would give my heart to Him but only if He gave her back to me. I confessed my sins and asked Jesus to come into my heart; my life as a follower of Jesus began.

I don't remember how it happened, but God held up His end of the bargain. We got back together and began counseling with the pastor who helped me. We ceased our sexual relationship and began attending church regularly. We began reading our Bibles together and memorizing scripture.

I got a call one evening and she told me we needed to talk about her past. I was afraid that she was going to break up with me and worried about what she had to say. I wanted to respond positively, so I prayed for God to give me a relevant Bible verse.

Let no unwholesome word proceed from your mouth, but only such a word as is good for edification according to the need of the moment, so that it will give grace to those who hear.
—Ephesians 4:29

She told me that she'd been married a few times before and felt I needed to know it. I felt betrayed because she hadn't told me earlier, but before I spoke, I remembered the scripture I'd memorized. Instead of yelling at her, I gently said, "That's okay. I'm glad you told me."

God was working in my life. I saw signs everywhere and became quite zealous about my faith, telling all my friends about it. God was real and I wanted them to know it!

We began talking about getting married. We still fought regularly, but as baby Christians, we saw God as a "magic pill" that we had swallowed and that He would solve all of our problems. Our dream for family was so strong that we became oblivious to the unhealthiness of our relationship. We ignored all of the warning signs (including a couple more acts of DV) that cautioned us against getting married.

One night I was lying on her couch, unable to fall asleep, wrestling with the decision of getting married or not. I picked up my Bible and asked God to give me an answer. Proverbs 15:22 caught my eye:

Plans fail for lack of counsel, but with many advisers they succeed.

I was so excited about the revelation that I rushed into her room and woke her up.

We decided to seek counsel from every Christian we knew. Almost every person I counseled with told me to marry her. Looking back on those conversations, I'm sure I left out some of the most important details about our relationship, only telling them what they needed to hear to convince me it was okay to get married.

I had a weeklong business trip planned in Arizona and asked her to join me for the week. She agreed.

We shopped for wedding rings, and she showed me the one she liked. The next day, I bought it before returning to our hotel room. Several days later, I proposed to her as the sun was coming up in the desert.

"Yes!" she said excitedly.

We were so excited about our newfound faith and our upcoming marriage that we decided we were going to share our faith with our family at our wedding, followed by being baptized in Lake Roosevelt.

Deep inside, I knew we shouldn't be getting married. An argument before our rehearsal dinner ruined what was supposed to be a special evening with family.

On our wedding day, I felt very uncomfortable. In the previous 2 months, we fought more often than when we enjoyed each other's company. On that day, she still had a week-old bruise on her arm from when I grabbed her during an intense argument.

But I ignored those feelings, believing in my heart that God was a magic pill and He would miraculously heal all of our problems when we got married.

But God didn't. We got into another argument as we were packing her things into the moving truck. She yelled at her older daughter, "Call the police! He's going to hurt me!"

I convinced her not to call and we finished packing the truck.

The next two and a half years were living hell. Yelling and screaming replaced the love and peace we'd occasionally experienced as a family while dating. When we were dating, we could get away from each other because I lived 4 hours away. When we were married, we couldn't get away from each other so the tension intensified. We both knew something would have to change.

We decided that having a baby would help us. Seven months later my wife was pregnant with our first daughter, Monica. Of course, a new baby did anything but help us. It brought more stress into our home. As anyone with a new baby can attest, they need attention in the middle of the night. With less sleep, our irritability was at an all-time high, culminating in the act of DV that sent me to jail.

We tried and tried to make our relationship work but things only got worse. We needed help, so we asked our pastor for guidance. His advice led us to weekly sessions with a marriage counselor.

After only a few short months of counseling, it became obvious that we needed to separate, so on January 8, 1999, I moved out of our house.

Six months later, our marriage counseling sessions had dwindled to 1 per month. Because of the terms of the protection order, we couldn't talk to each other on the phone or see each other. I was now living in Bob's back yard in my motor home and feeling very emotionally healthy.

One summer evening, I was riding in Bob's suburban, sitting in the back seat chatting with Bob and his wife. My cell phone rang and I answered it. It was my wife's older daughter.

"Damon, I've got something to tell you," she said.

"Okay, what is it?" I responded.

"Mom is never home. I think she's seeing someone," she said.

I was crushed. Once again, I was being abandoned. I was flooded with those same emotions that I'd experienced too many times in my 31 years. I thanked Trista for telling me and we hung up.

I shared what I'd heard with Bob and his wife. If what Trista had said was true, I couldn't do anything about it. I couldn't call my wife to confirm it. I couldn't visit the house to see if it was true. I was completely powerless, and this situation was out of my control.

For days afterward, I could think of nothing else. In my entire adult life, I'd never felt so hurt and abandoned. I became bitter and angry, but I couldn't share these feelings with my wife. Fortunately, Bob and Steve were there and listened as I wept. There was nothing they could do, either, except pray with me.

In the next few months, I became closer to God than I'd been in my entire life. I would wake every morning and drop to my knees, pleading with Him to take away my pain and reconcile our marriage; but He didn't.

God wanted to permanently heal my DV. He knew what I needed, and He loved me enough to give it to me. I needed to be in a position where I had no control of the outcome and had to rely solely on Him for my strength, and He put me in that position. It would be nearly 4 years and dozens of hours of counseling before I finally fully surrendered control of our relationship to God.

A friend recommended the book *Love Must Be Tough*, by

James Dobson. I read it and knew what to do. I wrote my wife a letter telling her that if she wanted to continue being married to me, she would have to end this other relationship. If she didn't do it by summer's end, I would file for divorce.

She didn't end it, so I filed for divorce and learned that there was a mandatory waiting period from the time of filing until the divorce was finalized. The next months were filled with times of high hope, followed by times of deep despair. I finally graduated from my DV class and the protection order was dropped.

We got together a number of times, but it would only take a few short days before our relationship deteriorated and we'd revert into the same pattern. During one of my personal counseling sessions, Pam said, "Damon, why do you continually put yourself in situations where you'll get crushed? It's like you have your head between a truck and a wall. The truck keeps backing up, crushing your head. Instead of walking away, you keep coming back for more."

In July of 2000, the pain of staying married was greater than the pain of getting a divorce, and so we were divorced.

I would get to see Monica 3 weekends a month and on Wednesdays. My ex-wife would continue living in the house until it was sold.

My dream of Monica growing up with her biological family intact seemed to be lost. God hates divorce, and now Monica would feel the pain of our poor choices.

But as much as I tried, I couldn't let go of my dream. Over the next 3 years, I would try everything humanly possible to make things work between us, but it would ultimately take what I believe was a small miracle to finally end our relationship for good.

Questions to Consider

- If you are dating, what red flags do you see in your relationship?
  - How will you address them before you get married?
- Do you have wise counselors in your life?
  - If not, what will you do to find them?
  - If so, what decisions can you bring to them for advice?
- Do you have a dream in your heart for family?
  - What do you need to do to ensure the dream will be realized?
- How can I help you?
  - You can find more resources and my contact information at **www.paindriveschange.com**.

8
The Pain of Reconciliation

All this is from God, who reconciled us to himself through
Christ and gave us the ministry of reconciliation:
that God was reconciling the world to himself in Christ,
not counting people's sins against them.
And he has committed to us the message of reconciliation.
—2 Corinthians 5:18-19

It was the hardest decision I had ever made. We had lived separate lives for a year and a half, and the time finally arrived when we had to move forward. I can't even count the number of times our relationship swung from incredible hope that we'd make it, to pure hopelessness that it would never work.

Dr. Jim Talley calls this *homeostasis* in his book *Reconcilable Differences.* After a couple is married, an "invisible rubber band" holds their lives together. When one person in the marriage pulls away, it draws the other person closer. Eventually, the tension from the invisible rubber band draws the person pulling away closer. Unfortunately, these "cycles" are rarely synchronized. When one person pulls away, the other isn't interested.

So, on July 12, 2000, our divorce became final. I didn't want a divorce, but the pain of remaining married was too great. My ex-wife's actions were not congruent with a desire to remain married, so I chose divorce.

These cycles continued even after the divorce, but I was done with our relationship and ready to get on with my life.

My pain from the failed attempts at reconciling was too great. My ex-wife sensed this and quickly began contacting me. It wasn't easy, but I resisted her attempts.

I was emotionally drained following our divorce. I went to work, sitting in my office staring out the window for hours, looking at the clock, counting the minutes until I could go to my apartment and go to sleep. There were many days when I couldn't make it the full 8 hours, so I took a few hours of vacation time and went home to sleep.

I wore my wedding ring until the day we divorced. Separation didn't give me the freedom to begin dating other women because I was still married, even if we didn't live together. It wasn't easy. One day while I was still married, I was shopping for a gift for Monica's birthday. A beautiful woman saw that I was struggling and asked me how old my daughter was. She told me that her daughter was the same age. We had a great conversation, and I felt myself strongly attracted to her. I asked her for her phone number and she gave it to me.

Later that evening, I fantasized about enjoying a healthy relationship with this beautiful woman. The more I thought about her, the more I wanted to call her. But I knew it would be wrong, and I reminded myself that men of integrity don't date when they are married.

I asked Bob to come out to my motorhome for a quick talk. I told him about her and I gave him her phone number, asking him to keep it just in case. That was the last time I saw her phone number.

I worked at Honeywell and became good friends with Dale and his wife. One time I was having dinner with them and Dale's wife told me about a woman she knew from church. She said she'd been divorced and had a young daughter just as I did. Her name was Debbie, and she taught Sunday school in her daughter's class at the church I formerly attended.

She said Debbie was not typical, she cleaned her own gutters, put up her own Christmas lights, and was very beautiful. Before I could say no she gave me Debbie's phone number. I was still married, I told her, but I tucked her number into my wallet.

There were plenty of days before we divorced when things weren't going well that I wanted to call that number. There is nothing like a beautiful woman to temporarily remove the pain of separation. But I didn't call her. I was married and men of integrity don't do that.

I did, however, call her after only 3 weeks of being divorced. I was still in deep pain, but I now had the freedom to begin new relationships. I really enjoyed our conversation and asked her if she'd like to go on a date. To my astonishment, she said she would enjoy that.

On August 14, 2000, only a month after my divorce, Monica and I pulled into Debbie's driveway. She lived in a neighborhood with clean streets—much like the place I'd written about in my dream a year and a half earlier.

I knocked on the door and Debbie answered it. Wow, I thought, she is beautiful! I still remember what she was wearing! Debbie's home was tidy and clean. When I entered, I felt a sense of peace that I hadn't experienced in a long time. Her smile was beautiful, her voice gentle.

Debbie's daughter, Amanda, walked out of her room with a beautiful smile as well. She was 6 at the time and Monica was 3. They went outside and started playing together while Debbie and I sat on her back porch getting to know each other. It was so easy to talk to her and she was incredibly gentle and peaceful. When she offered Monica something to drink, I felt the dream of family coming to life in my heart. She would be a great stepmom for Monica, I thought to myself.

We decided to go to the Bite of Edmonds together that day. We enjoyed each other so much that I invited her to go see the *Jesus of Nazareth* outdoor play that evening. She hesitated for a moment and then said, "Yes, I'd love to."

We shared a faith and love for Jesus and began building a foundation on our first date. That evening as we drove home, the wind blew through Monica and Amanda's hair in the back seat of my Toyota Forerunner. It was a cool summer evening and I had the top off. We arrived at her home and said goodbye, knowing that we'd be seeing each other again.

I wrote in my journal, "Wow, what an incredible lady. I look forward to getting to know her."

We began by spending time together and becoming friends. She had been divorced for 4 years and knew that the pain of my divorce was too fresh, so we agreed to be friends. She knew it was too soon; I didn't. Being with her took away all the pain I felt from my divorce.

We spent hours together talking about our previous marriages and discovered that we shared a common deep hurt. Divorce had taken away our hope of raising our children with an intact family. One day, I was in her house and began browsing through her bookshelf. As I looked through the titles, I was amazed at the similarities between the books she was reading and those I was reading. Books like *Dating with Integrity; Saving Your Second Marriage Before It Starts;* and *Love Must Be Tough.*

Bob had told me years earlier that the person you become will be shaped by the books you read and the people you associate with. Debbie and I were likeminded, and it showed through our choices of books to read.

My ex-wife learned that I had a new female friend, and she didn't like it. She would call me and tell me how much she missed me and wanted me back. But at this point, I didn't want her back. Debbie was amazing and I wanted to honor her by avoiding conversations with my ex. I firmly asked her to stop calling me because we were divorced and I had moved on.

Debbie and I continued seeing each other. On September 12, 2000, I wrote "Great date last night. I found myself very attracted (physically, emotionally, and spiritually)." Every one of my journal entries described how great our times were together.

One of the books I'd read recommended building a prioritized list of the attributes you'd want in a future spouse. I had built a list of thirty-two attributes. After only 2 months of knowing her, it was becoming more and more obvious that Debbie had most of these attributes.

On October 6, I took Debbie out to celebrate her birthday at Cucina Cucina, an Italian restaurant with butcher paper for tablecloths. Taking out a crayon, I demonstrated my theory on why we got along so well together. John Maxwell, in his book, *The 21 Irrefutable Laws of Leadership*, teaches about the *Law of Magnetism*, which states, "We attract who we are." I told her that she was 1 in a million—geeking out a little bit by drawing a bell-shaped curve and teaching her a bit about what I did for a living as a Six Sigma Master Black Belt. I then affectionately called her my "Six Sigma Girl."

I then boasted a little bit and said that I, too, was unique. Since we were both so unique, I explained, the Law of Magnetism dictated that we would be attracted to each other. She really enjoyed this and folded up the butcher paper to keep it.

A short week later, as we were taking a walk together, I told her that I was going to marry her one day.

I invited Debbie and her daughter to join Monica and me for a hike a few days later. Monica and I would be camping in my motorhome at the North Cascades and she could meet us on our way home. We started hiking toward the Ice Caves, and I watched Debbie treat Monica like she was her own daughter, loving her, holding her hand, and laughing as the 3 of them hiked.

Immediately, I felt a deep emotional pain, a pain that I hadn't felt in months. This made no sense, I told myself. Debbie is perfect, she's not abandoning me, so why am I feeling this way?

We hiked back down to the motorhome and Debbie made us lunch. As we sat down to pray, I once again felt that deep pain. Debbie knew something wasn't right with me as she felt me pulling away from her emotionally.

The next evening, just 7 days after I'd told her that I was going to marry her someday, I called her and told her we needed to talk. I drove the motorhome to her house and asked her to come in. I shared with her how much I cared for her and how incredible she was. I told her about the pain I'd felt the day before as I watched her loving Monica like her mommy. I told her that in those moments, I realized I wasn't ready for Monica to have a new mommy. My dream hadn't died of having Monica grow up with her biological mommy and daddy. As much as I wanted to move forward and continue our relationship, I couldn't. That invisible rubber band that Dr. Jim Talley talked about was pulling me back toward my ex-wife. I would need to either reconcile my relationship and re-marry her or permanently extinguish this dream.

"I'm sorry, Debbie. You are an incredible woman," I said.

With tears in her eyes she said, "I understand. This is the right thing to do and I'd do the same thing if I were in your situation. Goodbye," and she walked out the door of my motorhome.

As I drove home that evening, I wondered if I'd made a mistake. I was leaving the woman of my dreams for what would become the nightmare of an attempted reconciliation.

I remembered the book, *Reconcilable Differences,* that I'd read only a few weeks after I'd separated from my wife. All of my life I've had an uncanny ability of developing relationships with the people that are the best in the world at what they do. If I was going to reconcile my relationship with my ex-wife, I'd ask Dr. Talley to guide me. I didn't know if he could or would guide me, but I was going to try. I found his phone number and gave him a call.

"Damon, I'd love to help you out," he told me. "I'm going to send you a workbook I wrote called *Reconciliation Instruction.* I can counsel you as you work through it; I charge $50 per session."

Seriously, I thought? $50 per session to be with the world's expert on reconciliation. "Absolutely!" I said. "Doesn't my ex-wife need to be a part of the process?"

"Yes, ideally," he said, "but she doesn't have to. I'll tell you ahead of time, Damon. This will be very hard, and most of the time it doesn't end in remarriage. The primary goal of reconciliation and my definition of reconciliation is to enable those who are angry, bitter, and hostile to be friendly again and bring back harmony. Are you sure you want to proceed?"

"Yes," I said with absolute conviction.

"Okay. Then you'll need to completely cease all communication with Debbie. You'll need to be 100% dedicated to your ex-wife for this process."

"Is there any other way?" I pleaded.

"No," he said. "You'll need to let her know before we talk again."

I called Debbie and told her that I was going to be following the Reconciliation Process and that we could no longer talk to each other or see each other. She didn't like this rule, and I didn't either, but I was committed to following the process and fully submitting to Dr. Talley's guidance. We both cried on the phone and said our goodbyes.

The next couple of months were very challenging for me. To make things worse, November through February are very dark and dreary in Seattle. I'd come home to my dark apartment after work and stare at the TV for hours trying to dull my pain. I slowly started talking with my ex-wife, sharing with her that I was going to be going through the reconciliation process.

"How will it work if I don't do it with you?" she asked.

"I don't know, I'm just doing exactly what Dr. Talley says. If you want to do it as well it would work better," I said.

She agreed to join me in the reconciliation process, so on January 3, 2001, we had our first conference call with Dr. Talley. The first step of the process required us to sign a commitment contract. The contract had a number of items that I didn't fully understand at the time, summarized below:

- Agree to meet together every other week for 8 sessions

- Do not discuss remarriage (this would protect the relationship from unrealistic expectations)

- Be willing to become mutually exclusive, no relational one-to-one time with anyone else of the opposite sex

- Even if the relationship breaks down, your commitment to reconciliation discussion must continue for the 8 sessions. This is to prevent either one of you from getting hurt, and to test your commitment level

- Agree to spend 10 hours together in the first month, 20 in the second, 30 in the third, and 40 in the fourth
- Physical involvement is to never exceed a French kiss. If it exceeds a French kiss, be willing to fill out the moral purity worksheet and contact our pastor within 24 hours

If you and your partner are both willing to accept the prerequisites and to commit yourselves to reconciliation discussion, sign and date both workbooks.

I made up my mind and immediately signed both of our workbooks. My ex-wife signed both workbooks as well and we began.

The premise of Dr. Talley's book is that the quality of a relationship is strongly correlated to the accumulated time you spend alone together (ATAT). I was to record our ATAT, and she was to record the quality of our time on a scale of one to ten.

In our first month, we spent ten hours together. We were attending the same church, and she had a home very close to the church, so I would visit she and Monica regularly. It was very enjoyable, and I began feeling the hope that we might actually reconcile!

In our second month, we spent twenty hours together. Things continued to improve and we began to enjoy each other's company again. During our counseling sessions, I found myself wanting to discuss hurts of the past, but Dr. Talley sternly told me not to discuss these issues.

My ex-wife's youngest daughter was struggling with addiction, and we found a Christian-based program in Minneapolis to help her recover. After she'd been in the program for a number of months we were invited to Minneapolis to visit her. This trip was the beginning of things going downhill for us.

The time together in Minneapolis, combined with the visits with her daughter were extremely emotional, and we felt like a family once again when we were together.

After we arrived home, I began distancing myself from my ex-wife and she began feeling abandoned. We quickly spiraled back into our old pattern of arguing, and our relationship deteriorated rapidly.

I later discovered that after I get emotionally close to a woman, I quickly distance myself and close my heart, and this is what I was doing with her.

I sensed that she was pulling away from me as well. I began to see signs that she wasn't honoring her commitment. On one of our phone calls, Dr. Talley reminded her of the rules we'd agreed to on the commitment and then firmly said, "Let's leave this one alone."

But I couldn't leave it alone. The same feelings of abandonment that had plagued me my entire life began creeping in. One afternoon I visited her at her home and she quickly asked me to leave. I didn't leave. I told her I couldn't believe she was violating her contract and asked her to think hard about what she was doing.

The next weeks and month were extremely painful. I didn't have proof that she was spending time with another man, but her behavior told me she was. I woke up in the middle of a nightmare one night and couldn't go back to sleep. I dreamt that we were getting a divorce again and that I experienced the same emotional pain as I did in our first divorce. I called her the next morning and asked her if she was seeing another man. She refused to answer me.

We hadn't finished the 8 sessions of *Reconciliation Instruction*. I wondered why I should continue the process— she didn't seem to be following through with her commitment so why should I?

I consulted trusted friends who knew my story. They encouraged me to back out of the contract. I was in deep pain and called Dr. Talley to tell him I was going to back out of my contract.

I'll never forget his response. "Damon, do you know what integrity is? Integrity means following through on your commitments. I'm not going to let you back out of this."

I begged him to let me out, but he wouldn't budge. He told me I had to remain available to her and to finish the process.

The next few months were challenging, but I matured because of the challenge: I was a man of integrity, and I would do what I said I was going to do.

I began journaling. In one journal, I wrote these words about my feelings:

- Scared-that my hopes of a future won't come to pass
- Lonely-like I don't have any friends
- Abandoned-like she no longer wants to be with me
- Betrayed-like we made a covenant and it isn't being held to
- Lied to-(maybe I am, maybe I'm not)
- Not valued
- Empty-like I put way too much expectation on the outcome of this relationship
- Unhealthy-like I'm so codependent that I still do this garbage
- Fragile-that such tiny things would knock me off kilter
- Curious-to know what the truth is
- Controlled-that someone else has such a grasp on my

emotions

- ◆ Controlling-that I would want to hold onto an unhealthy relationship because, I can "Fix It."

Clearly, I was in deep pain and needed help. I cried out to God, asking Him to take the pain away. He didn't. I slept to avoid the pain. Sleep didn't help. I could not escape the fear that consumed my mind and heart.

A friend gave me the book *Secrets of the Vine,* telling me that it might help me. As I was sitting in pain, I began reading the book. It told about John 15, verses 1 and 2:

I am the true vine, and my Father is the gardener. He cuts off every branch in me that bears no fruit, while every branch that does bear fruit he prunes so that it will be even more fruitful.

I believe God spoke to me through this book, specifically about the difference between being disciplined by God and being pruned. Discipline happens when you're doing something *wrong.* For example, my DV was *wrong* and God disciplined me. Through His discipline I began to bear fruit in my life. Pruning happens when you're doing something *right.* For example, the men's group I led was *right* and was bearing fruit through these men's changed lives.

"That's it," I thought to myself! I know why I'm experiencing this deep pain. God is pruning me because I'm bearing fruit in my life! My ex-wife was the branch that needed pruning and He had taken out the pruning shears. This branch was not bearing any fruit and God needed to prune it away so that my life could be even more fruitful!

After seeing this, a sense of peace overcame me, the peace of God that transcends all understanding. I now understood why I was experiencing my deep pain, and this gave me the strength to continue. *I can do this,* I said! *I'm going to do this!*

Writing in my journal, I remarked that my purpose with

the reconciliation is: *When I meet my Maker, I want to say with 100% integrity that I gave this marriage and relationship everything I had. Ideally, He will reward that effort with a reconciled marriage. If not, he will still reward me because I acted with the highest of integrity and gave it everything a man could give.*

I met with Dr. Talley a few more times, and I completed the reconciliation process. He recommended that I write my ex-wife a note to officially close this chapter of my life.

I've reproduced this letter below:

My Letter to my Ex-Wife

August 20, 2001

We've known each other for 6 ½ years now. During that time, we've been through more than many people will ever experience in their lifetime. God has taken these circumstances to mold me into a stronger man. While I wouldn't ever want to go back and experience these things again, I wouldn't trade the blessings that have come as a result for anything in the world.

You are a very beautiful woman. You have a heart that desires to serve and to help others in need. You have a passion for raising your children to have a better life than you did. You have a conviction to be the best you can be, regardless of the circumstances.

I have loved you and still love you through the good times and the bad times. During our reconciliation, I gained a new respect for you, one that I had never enjoyed. I watched God do a marvelous work in you.

I want to ask your forgiveness. Primarily, your forgiveness for the inconsistent ways that I treated and loved you during our relationship. You said, "I felt like a rubber band." Well, that's because I treated you like a rubber band. When you got close to me, I'd push you away and when you were away, I'd draw you close to me. I'm sorry. Please forgive me.

I also want to ask your forgiveness for the abuse I put you and the girls through. Not only the physical abuse, but also the verbal and emotional abuse. I'm very sorry for the controlling behavior and specifically my inability to give you the freedom to be the woman that you are versus the woman I wanted you to be or thought you should be.

I want to ask your forgiveness for instilling a false hope about our future, about you and me re-marrying. I violated my own integrity and word, something I work very hard to maintain.

Finally, I want to ask your forgiveness for judging you and for not forgiving you for the things you've done to damage me. I still carry a 'millstone' around my neck, but am striving to let it go.

After divorcing you, I still held on to the hope that we would re-marry. During the reconciliation, I held onto the same hope. Even after I heard about your other relationship I hoped that we would one day be back together. Today, however, I know that it will never be. There comes a point in everyone's life when they must say "Enough." For me, that point came when we left your daughter in Minneapolis. That day, God gave me the peace I've been looking for since we separated in 1999. He said, "You've done all that I have asked; you are now free to go on with your life." This has since been confirmed numerous times through reading the Bible, counseling, reading books, and in prayer.

So, I am now moving forward with my life. I am closing the door on our relationship; this chapter of my life is now over. As the scripture says, 'I am forgetting what lies behind.' This wasn't an easy decision to make. In the process I've had to let go of my dreams of the future we shared. I know God has great things in store for you and great things in store for me. I still pray for you daily, and truly wish the best for you and your future.

As for me, I am very wounded. I wish that I could say that seeing you doesn't affect me, but it does. Talking with you affects me, voice messages affect me, hearing Monica talk about you affects me, and dropping her off in the morning affects me. I am wounded, and I recognize that you, too, are wounded. I furthermore recognize that you are dealing with your pain in a different way than I am.

I counseled with Pastor Ross, Dr. Talley, and Pam independently, asking each what they felt was most prudent to expedite my own healing. They all gave me the same answer. "Time heals all wounds." More specifically, they each felt that any communication (in person or on the phone) would only hinder the healing.

Pastor Ross recommended that we not see or talk to each other for a minimum of ninety days. Dr. Talley and Pam both agreed, this would be a good time to "de-toxify." Pastor Ross furthermore recommended the use of North Seattle Pre-School for drop off and pick up of Monica. I knew God was behind this when you called 2 hours later and said you wanted to start Monica in pre-school at North Seattle!

Thank you in advance for respecting my wishes and allowing me to heal and close this chapter of my life. I am going to take this time to "de-toxify" from my negative emotions and with God's help, forgive you.

As for our future, we must realize that God has given us a special gift in Monica. I hope we can remain focused on raising her with the morals and values that God would desire her to have.

—*Damon*

Two and a half years after we separated, I finally had the peace I was so desperately searching for. I was able to let go of my dream of raising Monica with her biological mom and dad and move on with my life. God knew what I needed to get here. He used a radio program to introduce me to *Reconcilable Differences*. He used Dr. Talley as a counselor, and He used my pain and fear of abandonment to draw me closer to Him. Moreover, He used his Word, the Bible, to reveal to me why I was feeling that pain. He was preparing me to bear more fruit throughout my life, and once again, He would use Dr. Talley and his wisdom to help me bear that fruit!

Questions to Consider

- Are there any relationships in your life that you need to reconcile?
  - What is your next step toward reconciliation?
- Are there areas of your life that aren't producing fruit?
  - How can you proactively prune these before experiencing pain?
- How can I help you?
  - You can find more resources and my contact information at **www.paindriveschange.com**.

9
The Pain of Generational Curses

*I lay the sins of the parents upon their children; the entire
family is affected—even children in the third and fourth
generations of those who reject me.*
—Exodus 20:5

God blessed me with a number of wise counselors in this
season of my life, and I was like a sponge. Pam was a
counselor from the church Bob attended. I decided to set up
an appointment with her. I shared my story and she revealed
that she specialized in addictions and co-dependency. Pam
was both wise and direct.

After only a few sessions, she said, "Damon, do you know
what a love addict is?"

"No," I responded, thinking it was some sort of joke.

"Damon, I think you struggle with love addiction. Let me
share a picture that summarizes what that is."

Pam pulled out a copy of Pia Melody's book "Facing
Love Addiction" and shared a picture that summarized love
addiction.

She explained that the greatest fear of a love addict is the
fear of abandonment with an underlying fear of intimacy.

"I've watched you go through this cycle multiple times. You
are attracted to your ex-wife's seductiveness, and you begin
feeling 'high' from the fantasy of being together. You begin
to feel relief from your pain of being alone. But then, you
become very needy. This neediness pushes your partner away
and triggers your fear of abandonment. In order to protect

yourself, you withdraw emotionally and begin finding other ways to eliminate this pain. Your withdrawal attracts your ex-wife and the cycle continues and continues," she said.

Pam was exactly right! This was the pattern of every dating relationship I'd ever encountered.

"What do I need to do to change it?" I asked.

"It will be very hard, Damon, but you can do it. We'll have to dig up the pains of the past and work through them. We'll go through a recovery work process."

We spent the next several months going through this process, and I uncovered many unresolved hurts. Pam eventually asked me to tell her about my mom. I shared my memories and my hurts.

"Damon," she said, "you have a lot of unresolved bitterness toward your mom. I'd recommend you write her a letter. You don't have to send her that letter, but write it and get all of your feelings of hurt and pain out in the open."

I took her advice and wrote Mom a letter. The more I wrote, the angrier I became. I began to see very strong similarities between she and my ex-wife—both had troubled relationships with their dads, both turned to men as comfort, both struggled with marital relationships, both struggled with anger, and both blamed others for their problems.

When I married my ex-wife, I "married" my mom! When I took on the responsibility of her children, I subconsciously thought I could "fix" my childhood by being their dad. But I couldn't fix them, and I couldn't fix our marriage. Letting go meant letting go of my childhood and the possibility that it could be fixed.

But you can't fix your childhood. I called Mom and told her what I had learned and told her about my anger towards her. I was hoping she would acknowledge my pain but she didn't. Instead, she blamed me and everyone else for her issues. She took no responsibility for her actions that had devastated her children and were now devastating my child.

In anger, I hung up the phone. Mom was treating me just as my ex-wife was treating me. This wasn't acceptable. I needed to set some boundaries, so I wrote her this letter:

My Letter to my Mom

Mom,

I'm not going to raise Monica like I was raised. That is one thing I realize for sure. I'm going to make the best of the situation, and give her a solid foundation. I hope you can understand and respect that.

In terms of how I feel? Extremely angry. I am having the same discussions with my father, and it isn't easy. I'm having to be firm with my ex-wife, and that isn't easy either. So why do I do it? Because it is the right thing, and I love each of you so much that I will no longer enable *our unhealthy relationships.*

I hope you understand. I want you to know, once again, that I do not blame you for my situation. I made my choices. I am, however, extremely angry and do not feel it is prudent to talk with you or see you. I'm not going to be over for Thanksgiving, and probably not Christmas either. I have to work through my feelings so that when I see you, I can be civil, not angry.

Feel free to write as often as you like. I do still love you.

Your son,

—Damon

Christmas was very important to Mom. This was the

one time of the year that she would get all of her children together. She couldn't afford to prepare a big dinner, so she saved all year for Christmas, and she spared no expense. She cooked prime rib, crab salad, shrimp salad, potatoes, multi-colored fruit salad, rolls as big as your fist, Jell-O salad, and pies. Christmas was indeed special for all of us, and the meal was fit for a king.

Be that as it may, my anger toward her was so great that I chose not to be there for Christmas, not to punish her but to set healthy boundaries so I could begin to heal.

At one counseling session, I told Pam about my relationship with my dad and how a counselor had helped me work through my anger with him. I asked her if she would do the same for my mom.

"Sure, but I doubt she'll come. I can count on 1 hand the number of parents that have been willing to come to counseling in my twenty-plus years as a professional," she said.

"I'll try," I said.

Much to my surprise, though, Mom agreed and came to spend a week with me. We would use this time to heal the wounds of the past.

When we began our first counseling session, Pam asked us to draw a picture of our dream for family. Mom drew a picture at Christmas with all of her kids smiling and opening presents near a fireplace. Her family was happy, warm, and together.

Interestingly enough, I drew the same picture.

I was beginning to understand Mom. I flooded her with questions.

"Did your parents know God?"

"No," she said.

Did your grandparents know God?

"No."

"Did they pray when she was a child?"

"No."

"Did we go to church as children?"

"Yes."

"Did Dad go to church with us?"

"I can't remember."

I asked her to explain how we started going to church.

She told me about how the neighbors "shined God's love and helped" when she needed help. This light made her want that. She wanted that type of family, so we started going to church. When no one else was there to help, the church was!

"Did we kids give our hearts to the Lord?"

"Yes, you did."

"Did you give your heart to the Lord?"

"Not right then, but I did later with my friend, Violet."

"Did Dad give his heart?"

"I don't know."

I then explained to her that the Bible says the sins of the fathers pass down from the third and fourth generations, and I was the fourth generation!

She attempted to explain what had happened when I was a child—how she'd been dreaming about our conversation in the days leading up to our counseling session. She began by explaining that I never really had family, and even as far back as when I was a baby, things were going south.

I then told her about some of my strongest memories before I was 3:

- The house being cold

- Starting a fire in the oven
- Going to Grandma and Grandpa's house and it being cold
- Dad telling us the family was getting divorced during breakfast
- Dad's small house during the separation

We talked at length about why I had such strong memories of being cold.

She said, "It was a cold winter. Dad was always gone at work, and I had to steal coal to warm the furnace."

I surmised that she and Dad had their strongest arguments about it being cold.

I asked her if she knew why I could so vividly recalled the fire I'd started in the oven.

"You were probably trying to protect your family by warming the house in the morning. Perhaps you could get Mommy and Daddy to stop fighting if you could warm the house."

This was so significant that when she told me this, I began to cry. As I write this, I am crying again.

To this day, I have the following strong personality traits:

- I protect my family, no matter what
- I believe I can solve any problem
- I work diligently to provide so my family won't do without

This was a major breakthrough for me. I thanked Mom and told her I loved her.

I then recalled a strong memory of getting my mouth stuck on a faucet. She told me this was a very traumatic thing. I had gotten my tooth stuck, and she had to pull my mouth off, and in the process pulled my front tooth out! She said she was very angry, and yelled at the top of her voice.

"That explains my behavior," I said! To this day, when a woman raises her voice at me, I have no tolerance and I immediately begin snapping back treating them very poorly.

We then began to focus on Mom. What had happened to her? She admitted that she began to go out and get attention from another man when Dad wasn't around. She was empty, and someone new made her feel good. She started drinking too much and went through many men. Along the way, she developed a serious mental illness.

Mom said she began to blame herself for all that happened in the marriage. She felt guilty about what happened.

I asked, "Have you forgiven yourself?"

She said, "No, I haven't."

We then talked about my brother Dean's death and how she'd gotten angry with God. I asked her if she'd forgiven God.

"No," she said, "I haven't! I feel like God was punishing me for doing bad things by taking my son away."

She said she used to call Grandma when she was hurting from her son's death and Grandma would say, "Just get busy."

I asked if Grandma ever said, "It's okay Marge. It's okay to feel this way." But Grandma never did.

I asked if she'd ever dealt with the pain. She said she hadn't, that she was afraid to feel, because whenever she would feel, her father would discipline her. And if she cried, he'd discipline her again.

I told her that I didn't believe God punishes people." I asked if she'd ever heard this as a child.

"Probably," was her answer.

I asked if she ever trusted anyone in her life.

She said, "Everyone I've ever trusted has betrayed me."

I then pointed out that if she couldn't trust those she could see, it would be hard to trust someone she couldn't see (God).

She agreed and wondered how she could trust and forgive God.

I just said, "It's okay, Mom. It's natural to feel the way you do. It's okay to feel, it's okay to be angry, I love you."

I told her that she was a great mom and I forgave her.

That week with Mom was the best week we've ever spent together. We played with Monica and shared delicious meals together. I showed her where I worked at Microsoft, and I spoiled her by taking her shopping.

During the week my hurt and anger towards mom was replaced with love and compassion, softening my hardened heart towards her. Mom's parents didn't know Jesus and raised her to the best of their abilities. When Mom was acting out, she needed to be disciplined in love, much like Steve had taught me a few years earlier. Instead of love, she received anger. When she expressed her feelings, she received more anger, so she learned how not to feel. Just as I was a product of my childhood, Mom, too, was a product of her childhood.

Over the months and years to come, Mom and I continued to build our relationship. She would come to visit and play with Monica while I went to work. We went salmon fishing on my boat, and she caught her first salmon. During our counseling session I decided that I was going to honor her, and I've tried to do so ever since.

"Honor your father and mother"—which is the first commandment with a promise— "so that it may go well with you and that you may enjoy long life on the earth."
—Ephesians 6:2-3

A few years later, I got a phone call from Mom. She was

talking very fast, sharing stories about how she was ready to go to heaven and meet her son. She said she had been sleeping only a few hours a night.

"Mom, are you manic?" I asked. Mom knew I had been diagnosed with bi-polar disorder but had never been evaluated herself.

"I don't think so," she said.

I called my sister who lived in Spokane and told her I was worried and that she might need to bring Mom to the hospital.

Later that evening, my sister called me and said she'd taken Mom to the hospital, and they admitted her to the psychiatric ward. I spoke with her doctor and shared that I was bipolar but Mom had never been diagnosed.

He told me that she "was having a manic episode," and he had diagnosed her with bipolar disorder. He said that it is hereditary and asked me what medication I took to manage it.

I told him that Depakote worked well for me, and he said he'd start her with it, but it would take a few days before she would come down from her manic state.

I visited Mom in the hospital a few days later. She was composed. She was more peaceful than she had been in a long time.

"Mom, you look great," I said.

"Thanks, I feel great," she responded.

I asked her why she was feeling so good, and she said that her diagnosis of bipolar disorder helped her put the pieces of her life together.

"This explains why as a teenager my dad tried and tried but couldn't get me to stop acting out. I was probably having a manic episode," she said. "This explains why the fights and arguments with your dad were so extreme. I was manic. This explains why I acted out when I was with your dad—I was manic."

I wish they could have diagnosed me when I was a teenager; it would have saved us from all of the pain we've gone through. I could see that she was deeply saddened but also deeply relieved. I told her it was okay and I forgave her—and so did Jesus.

Mom stayed in the hospital through Thanksgiving. We brought her Thanksgiving dinner and enjoyed it with her, giving thanks that God had finally revealed her bipolar disorder and that she was now being treated for it.

I had been attending church at the same church that my ex-wife attended. We went to different services and rarely saw each other. Don, the pastor of the church, knew both of us and played an instrumental role in my personal recovery helping me grow into the man I am today. I attended his church for more than ten years, and Don discipled me like he would a son.

Don preached a sermon during one of the first services I attended on addictions called "Taming the Dragon Within." It was God's timing because I was going through addiction counseling, and I was also preparing a course called "Understanding Addictions" that I taught at Prisoners for Christ, a ministry that I was heavily involved with.

I met with Don and told him about my counseling, the course I was teaching, and I thanked him for his great sermon. He shared his story and I knew I could trust him. Don recommended the book *Love is a Choice,* by Robert Hemfelt, Frank Minirth, and Paul Meier. Don said this was the best book he'd read on addictions in twenty-five years and recommended that I read it.

I picked up the book and quickly learned why he'd recommended it. This book perfectly described me, as well as my childhood experiences! After reading the book I understood exactly why my mom and dad had married, and it explained why I chose and married my first wife. After seeing a similar diagram in the book I created these diagrams.

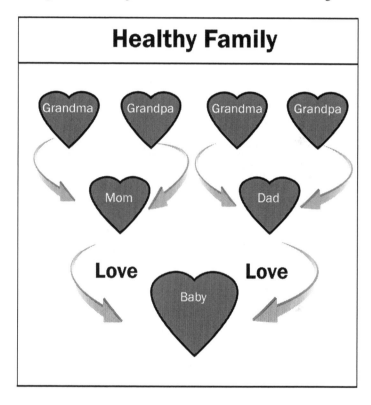

In healthy families, parents are full of love, and they give that love to their children, filling their "heart tank." When these children grow up, they are attracted to people similar to themselves and marry people with full "heart tanks." When they have children, they are so full of love that they fill the child's "heart tank" with love. The child grows up and the cycle continues for generations.

In unhealthy families; however, the parents have empty heart tanks. They are attracted to people with empty heart tanks as well. When they marry, they look to each other to fill their heart tanks. But 2 halves don't make a whole, so they struggle in their marriage.

When they have children, they don't have enough love in their heart tanks to fill the babies' heart tank. Instead of filling their child's heart they drain love from the child, leaving its heart tank empty. The child grows up and the cycle continues for generations.

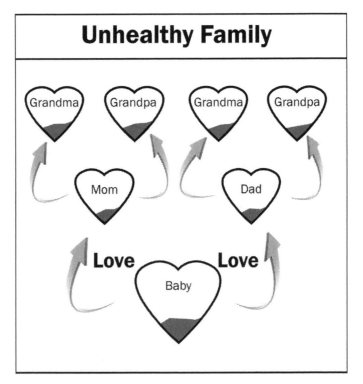

WOW! This is why I was attracted to and married my first wife! This is why Mom and Dad married! This is why our marriage struggled and why their marriage struggled. This is why I looked to women to fill my void. My heart tank was empty and needed to be filled, so I chose women to try to fill it. But when they didn't, I was left feeling empty and tried harder to get them to fill it. This only pushed them away and triggered my feelings of abandonment, further draining my heart tank.

This one picture transformed my thinking and put all the pieces together. Now I understood the root of my behaviors and my issues. I understood what I'd need to do as a father to minimize the likelihood that Monica would be unhealthy as an adult and attract an unhealthy spouse. I understood how the generational curses had started, and I understood what would have to transpire to stop them.

Ending the generational curses meant that I would need to fill my heart tank and keep it full. By doing so, I would attract a woman with a full heart tank, and we would raise children with full heart tanks.

I am a problem-solver. I've always liked solving problems, and I've devoted my career to being a professional problem-solver. Learning how to break the generational curses was the biggest problem I'd ever attempted to solve in my life. This insight fueled my recovery.

I devoured books on addiction, relationships, parenting, and forgiveness. I counseled with multiple counselors every month. I taught courses on addiction. I attended a men's group called "Joshua's Men" and surrounded myself with other men that wanted to be better men. I went to parenting seminars and relationship seminars. I attended church in the mornings and asked for prayer at the altar for healing. I went to church in the evening to worship God and fill my heart with his love.

Those who knew me during this season of my life told me they saw "exponential growth" in me. I led the men's ministry at my new church, and I started a new Joshua's Men group. God had given a gift to me, and I wanted to pass it to others.

I was healthy and I had a support system in place to ensure that I stayed that way. I had the good fortune of many wise, trustworthy counselors in my life to guide me. My church was strong, as was my relationship with my pastor. I had forgiven my parents and I'd developed a deeper relationship with each of them. I had graduated from my DV class and hadn't committed any acts of DV in a couple of years. My bipolar disorder was firmly under control, and my moods were stable.

Through Dr. Talley's *Reconciliation Instruction*, I'd worked through the pain with my first wife, and I had relinquished my dream of ever remarrying her.

I was ready to start a new chapter of my life.

Questions to Consider

- Do you have unhealed wounds from your childhood?
  - What can you do to heal these wounds?
- Is your "heart tank" full or empty?
  - What are you doing to continuously fill it?
- Are you pouring love into your children to keep their heart tanks full?
  - How can you pour even more love into them?
- How can I help you?
  - You can find more resources and my contact information at **www.paindriveschange.com**.

10
The Joy of Healthy Dating

For it is God's will that you should be holy: You must abstain
from sexual immorality; each of you must know how to control
his own body in holiness and honor.
—1 Thessalonians 4:3-4

September is my favorite month. I love the beautiful fall
colors of the leaves on the trees, football season, and the
cool crisp air in the morning. It was Labor Day weekend in
2001, and my dad came over to spend some time together.
We went driving in my Toyota 4Runner, and I noticed a yard
sale sign. I love yard sales, and this sign pointed toward the
neighborhood that Debbie lived in.

My heart skipped a beat, and I subconsciously hoped that
Debbie was having a yard sale. I turned into the neighborhood
and the next sign pointed down the road to her house. I
drove up the road and was elated when I saw things for sale
in Debbie's yard!

"Dad, Debbie's having a yard sale. Let's go!" I said, as I
quickly parked the 4Runner and jumped out.

I hadn't seen Debbie in almost a year. We had both
honored the rules of the *Reconcilable Differences* process and
had both let go of the possibility that we'd be together again.
I'll be honest, I thought about Debbie quite often during
that year, especially when things weren't going well with my
attempted reconciliation, but I honored the rules.

I had accomplished my part and maintained my integrity
through the process. I was healthier than I'd ever been, and

I was now free to pursue new relationships. I had no desire to pursue other relationships, however. I had spent 3 months with Debbie, and I was convinced that she offered everything I had ever wanted in a future spouse.

I ran across the street and said hello, not knowing what to expect. She looked at me and smiled. She looked beautiful and I could feel my heart racing as we talked and updated each other.

I told her that I completed the reconciliation process and that I was ready to move forward. Debbie seemed pleased to hear that—she didn't think she'd ever see me again.

I took a chance and gave her my email address, asking her to email me so we could slowly become re-acquainted through email. Truth be told, I knew Debbie didn't spend much time on her computer and knew that if I received an email back it meant she was interested in getting re-acquainted. We hugged and I got back into my car with Dad.

As we drove away, I said, "Dad, I'm going to marry her! She is awesome."

We went to a few more yard sales and then headed home. I was anxious to see if she'd written me an email! I headed upstairs and quickly opened my laptop. To my surprise, I had a new email in my inbox from Debbie!

Over the next few weeks, we emailed each other back and forth and I began calling her. I'd made many mistakes in previous dating relationships, so I wanted to do this one right. I pulled out the list of the attributes I wanted in a future wife and re-prioritized them. I then put a checkmark on the list for each attribute Debbie had. There were thirty-two attributes, and Debbie had thirty-one of them. The last attribute, "willing to homeschool our kids" was a question mark because I didn't know for sure.

Attribute	Debbie
Godly	✓
Commited	✓
Accountable	✓
Selfless	✓
Giving	✓
Caring	✓
Soft	✓
Serving	✓
Secure	✓
Loving	✓
Physical Attractive (Body, Skin, Beauty)	✓
Compassionate	✓
Solid family life (Mom & Dad married entire life)	✓
Self-Confident	✓
....	

One of my favorite quotes is from W. Edwards Deming, considered by many as the father of the modern quality movement. A Japanese manufacturing company hired Deming after World War II to help them improve their quality problems. The management asked him to assess their people and processes and make recommendations for improving quality.

The managers fully expected Deming to recommend firing the bad employees, but Deming didn't make that recommendation. Instead, he counseled them that their processes were inconsistent, so they were producing poor results. If they wanted to improve quality, they would have to improve their processes.

> *Your system is perfectly designed to get you the*
> *results you are getting.*
> —Deming

The Japanese management listened to him and applied his principles, methodically modifying and overhauling their processes. Today, when we think about products built in Japan, we automatically think about their high quality. Deming is largely responsible for this.

When I thought about my personal life and my failures in dating, it would have been easy to blame the problems on the women I dated. But I didn't, I looked at my failures and realized that my dating "system" was perfectly designed to get me the results I'd gotten. If I wanted different results, I'd have to use a different "system."

Fortunately, I knew of a different dating system. Dr. Talley recommended I read his book, *Too Close Too Soon*. The underlying principle of this book is that the quality of a relationship is strongly correlated with the amount of accumulated time alone together. If you want to improve the quality of a relationship, improve the amount of time you spend alone together.

However, too much time alone together in the beginning of a relationship leads to physical involvement and stunts the emotional growth of the relationship. By minimizing the time alone together in the beginning, it will be easier to build a foundation of trust in the relationship.

I trusted Dr. Talley as he had guided me through the reconciliation process. Furthermore, I'd never had a relationship built on trust and always got "too close too soon" in my previous relationships. I decided to try it.

In early September, the salmon swim into the Puget Sound on their way to the rivers where they spawn. One afternoon I took my fishing boat out to see if I could catch a few. I got lucky and caught one. I called Debbie and asked her if she would like to have a barbecue that evening and offered my freshly caught salmon if she'd do the rest. She agreed.

I barbecued the salmon on her grill, and she prepared the trimmings to go with it. We had a great dinner together and decided to attend church together that Sunday. We quickly found ourselves enjoying each other's company, and our natural tendencies were to spend more time together.

I told her about Dr. Talley's book and that I didn't want to make the same mistakes I'd made previously. I told her it was really weird, but I wanted to follow his process and asked her if she'd be open to trying it with me.

She briefly hesitated then said, "Yes."

Neither of us fully knew what we were getting into, but we wanted our relationship to work and so we began.

The process required us to limit our time to twelve hours alone together in the first month, eighteen the second month, twenty-five the third month, and finally, thirty-five the fourth month, for a total of ninety hours over the 4-month period.

I had been tracking our time alone together since my first phone call to her after seeing her at the yard sale. When I totaled the time up, we'd already seen each other for fifteen hours and had exceeded the recommended twelve hours. We agreed to move the goal for the first month to twenty hours, knowing that we had 3 weeks to go but only 5 hours left in which to see each other.

Fortunately, Dr. Talley only requires you to count phone time if it exceeds thirty minutes, and time in a group of people could be divided by 4. I told Debbie we'd have to limit our one-to-one time, but that we could talk on the phone, go to church together, and hang out with our kids together.

As hard as we tried, we didn't meet our goal of twenty hours in the first month, our natural tendencies kicked in and we spent thirty-five hours total our first month. We decided to re-set the clock and agreed that we would limit the next month to eighteen hours, the following to twenty-five hours, the following to thirty-five, and the fourth month to fifty, understanding that this would force us to slow down, but also recognizing that after the second month it would get much easier.

We loved being together but desperately wanted our relationship to work out, so we agreed. I told her I would begin graphing our time in Excel and not to be surprised if I suddenly stopped contacting her. I had a measurable goal, and I was going to meet it, no matter what!

On our first night together after setting this goal, we did an exercise together that I would recommend every dating couple do. I handed Debbie a stack of yellow sticky notes and asked her to write out everything she wanted from a dating relationship, with 1 idea per sticky.

I then asked her to prioritize the sticky notes from the most important to the least important. After doing that, I asked her to rate our relationship on a scale of 1-10. This was a very powerful exercise for us because we quickly discovered that our relationship scored very high on the things that were most important to her! We both knew that we had a good thing going, and this exercise made it very clear for us both to see.

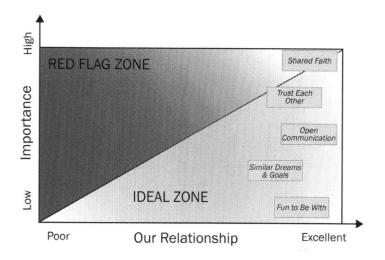

I looked at the clock and discovered we'd been together for 6 hours. We were enjoying our time so much that I didn't want to leave. I felt as if I had a giant rubber band around my waist, and as I started to leave, it would pull me back to spend more time with Debbie.

But we had made a commitment. I mustered up enough energy and told Debbie I didn't want to, but I had to leave. I reminded her that we had twenty-nine days left in the month and that we'd have to slow down.

The next time we met, we realized that spending 6 hours alone together was compromising our commitment. Furthermore, we realized that we needed to put some physical boundaries on ourselves to protect our sexual integrity. We'd discovered that being alone after eleven in the evening put us at risk so we agreed not to. A few weeks earlier we discovered that being alone for more than 5 hours put us at risk so we set this boundary as well. We agreed not to drink more than 1 drink when alone together, and finally we agreed to follow the time boundaries recommended by Dr. Talley. We included the activities we'd do together and wrote shared goals. We summarized all of this in a commitment contract and decided to ask our counselor to read it and hold us accountable.

It turned out that, Pam, my counselor, was Debbie's counselor as well, so we attended a joint counseling session to talk about our desires to maintain sexual purity and build a relationship with a foundation of trust. Pam agreed with the boundaries we had established and we all signed the contract together.

Afterwards, Pam looked at us both and gave our relationship her blessing, remarking that we were very well matched. Pam repeated the importance of maintaining our integrity throughout the process, reminding us of what Jesus said in Matthew 5:37:

Simply let your "Yes" be "Yes," and your "No," "No."...

After meeting with Pam and signing the contract with Debbie I had a strong sense of hope, but I also experienced a lot of peace. For the first time in my life, I had a deliberate plan to build a healthy relationship. This plan was measurable and based on Scriptural truths. The plan was predictable, and predictability brought me peace.

The next couple of months together were incredible. We both had young children and wanted to raise them to love Jesus, so we attended a parenting seminar together. We both struggled with co-dependency and attended a Boundaries seminar together. We went to church together, and we spent time with our friends. We went to a pumpkin patch together and carved a pumpkin with the kids and my mom.

Debbie quickly won my mom's heart and gave her a children's book about pumpkins as a memento of our time together. I gave Mom a picture of Debbie and me together at the pumpkin patch, which she hung on her wall.

"Mom, I'm going to marry her one day," I told her.

She looked at me and said, "Don't let her slip away, Damon. I've always prayed that God would bring a woman like her into your life. You deserve her."

We quickly learned how to maximize the limited time we had together. As I mentioned earlier, group time is divided by 4. That means that if we spend 8 hours together at a parenting seminar, we only had to count it as 2 hours against our allocated time for the month!

I recorded our time together and graphed it against our goal. Every time we began exceeding our goal, I would tell Debbie that we needed to slow down. One evening, we were alone at her house, snuggling on her couch watching a movie. I was feeling very connected to her as I felt the warmth of her body next to mine. We were deeply connected spiritually, were growing closer intellectually through the books and seminars we attended, and we were getting very close emotionally.

I didn't want to leave, and she didn't want me to leave. We hadn't kissed yet, but I knew that if I stayed much longer, we would kiss. I also knew that we wouldn't be able to stop there because we were "hugging the line" in terms of the time we'd spent together. We both were committed to maintaining our integrity.

I got up and told her it was definitely time for me to leave, so reluctantly, we said our goodbyes.

I drove home, knowing that the boundaries we'd put in place were protecting us from doing anything that would damage our long-term relationship.

This happened often over the next few months, and each time I was able to pull away because of the boundaries we'd established. I can honestly say that if we hadn't put these boundaries in place and limited our time alone together, we would have slipped into a sexual relationship outside of marriage violating our desires of sexual purity before marriage.

But we didn't slip. We kept building on our foundation and were growing closer and closer.

It was Thanksgiving, and I planned to drive to see my mom in Eastern Washington. I got into my car, but it wouldn't start. I didn't want to be alone on Thanksgiving, so I called Debbie. She told me she was having Thanksgiving with her parents and invited me up.

Deb's parents had been married for nearly forty years and lived in a spacious house only a few miles from my house. Spending time with them at Thanksgiving made me understand why Debbie was such an incredible woman. They were kind, generous, and they didn't judge me for being divorced. Debbie's mom was an incredible cook, and we enjoyed dinner together.

Later that evening, I went to Debbie's house. I reminded her that our families were completely different. She'd grown up in a stable home with a mom and dad that loved each other. She always had breakfast at 7:30 a.m., lunch at noon, and dinner at 6:00. When she was younger, she always went to bed at 8:15. *Consistency, predictability,* and *security* are the words I used to describe her childhood.

My childhood was exactly the opposite, Mom and Dad were divorced, chaos was the norm, and only rarely did I experience security.

I asked Debbie if she was sure that she wanted to be with me. My entire life was a mess, and her entire life seemed perfect. Debbie reassured me that her life wasn't perfect. She didn't care about my past, she was with me because of who I was as a man. I asked her to share how she was feeling at the time.

Debbie's Letter

My friends thought I was crazy! They had never heard of dating the way Damon was suggesting. A couple of them commented that it was like following a bunch of rules instead of 'feeling' or being in a relationship.

For me, though, it offered a strange sense of peace. I had been hurt by my first husband and every guy I dated just seemed superficial and eager for physical attention, but I just wasn't interested. Damon piqued my curiosity. Was he really willing to forego a physical relationship in order to get to know me? To build a friendship? It brought me an emotional safety that I had never experienced with the guys I dated. Sure, it was a little weird at first, but honestly, I felt taken care of. He was a leader and a man of integrity by following this process. He wanted to do the right thing and do it God's way. How could I not be attracted to that? (Plus, he was pretty handsome!)

Following the *Too Close Too Soon* process had protected my heart from being too enmeshed in the relationship. It also allowed us the time to take things slowly and really 'unpack' the issues we had and understand them. And there were many issues that came up! As he has shared in his book, he has a much different background than I do. A lot of his behaviors were remnants of his past. I knew he was working through them because he was very honest and vulnerable with me which established a very high level of trust with one another.

—Debbie

Even though I heard her words, doubts entered my mind, telling me that I didn't deserve a woman like her. So far, in our relationship, we had a few minor arguments, but we worked our way through them, and they even brought us closer together.

It was now January. We'd been dating for nearly 4 months, even though we had known each other for almost a year and a half. We hadn't kissed yet, but we cared deeply for each other, and I was ready to take our relationship to the next level.

After enjoying a delicious dinner together, I put some romantic music on. We turned the lights down and began dancing together, holding each other closely. I gazed into her eyes, and we kissed for the first time.

A few hours later, we were still kissing and struggling to stop. I once again thought about our boundaries and the commitment we had signed. Somehow, I was able to tell her that I needed to go. We kissed goodbye, and I drove home, excited that we just started a new phase of our relationship.

As I mentioned earlier, one of the requirements for *Too Close Too Soon* was that I would record the time we spent together, and Debbie would record the quality of our time together on a scale of 1-10. I hadn't received a "10," and we used to joke about it.

I asked her, "How about last night, did I get a 10?"

She smiled and said, "You know me, I'm never extreme. I'll give you a 9."

We continued growing closer to one another, going to church together and attending a marriage seminar. A friend watched as our relationship blossomed; he was so impressed that he asked me to teach a seminar at his church on dating relationships!

But our relationship wasn't perfect. We argued occasionally, and I found myself pulling away from her emotionally after our first kiss. My underlying fear of intimacy put a wall around my heart as a protective mechanism.

I was about to leave to teach a class in Phoenix, and I planned to be gone for a week. Debbie drove me to the airport. I had been treating her poorly for a few days, and the break from each other would give us a chance to figure out why I was acting that way.

It only took a few days before I realized what a jerk I had been, so I decided to make it up to her. I flew home a day early on Valentine's Day. I called her and asked her to get dressed up and meet me at the airport. We were going to celebrate our first Valentine's Day together!

When she arrived at the airport, I greeted her with a dozen roses and a sincere apology. We went out to our favorite steakhouse for a leisurely feast and afterwards, we spent hours together kissing and talking to each other.

Certainly, I thought, this date would rate me a 10.

"9.5," Debbie said with a big smile.

Unfortunately, whenever we'd get close, I would pull away. We had completed the first phase of *Too Close Too Soon*, and I no longer felt the protection that this process provided. I trusted it, but now that the first phase was complete, I would have to place this trust in our relationship. I trusted Debbie and we had built a foundation, but without the protection of the process, I was floundering, which caused Debbie to feel emotionally abandoned.

I had to return to Arizona for a meeting, and I asked Debbie to fly down and join me. I planned a very special date for our last evening together.

On March 17, 2002, we went out to a romantic Italian restaurant with a sensational view of the desert sunset. We enjoyed a bottle of wine together and an enjoyable conversation.

I gazed into her eyes and said, "Debbie, I love you."

She responded in kind, "I love you too, Damon."

This was the first time we'd acknowledged that we loved each other. We were both overwhelmed with joy and slept in the same bed that evening. We didn't have sex, but every fiber of our bodies longed to.

By sleeping in the same bed, though, we had thrust ourselves into a difficult situation that could have easily resulted in both of us violating our commitment that we remain pure until we were married.

Later, on a counseling call with Dr. Talley, we asked for advice about sleeping in the same bed before we were married. He gave us some advice that gave us the all the conviction we needed. "Do you have unsaved neighbors?"

"Of course," we both responded.

"Non-Christians are watching you," he said, "and looking for an excuse to discount your faith. If you spend the night at Debbie's house, what will they think when they see you walk out the door the next day? They have no way of knowing whether or not you had sex but they definitely know that you aren't married and will assume that you did have sex. You've just lost any hope of being able to win them to Christ."

After that weekend, Debbie and I never spent the whole night together in bed. We came close a couple of times when I fell asleep on her bed, though.

When we went camping together in my motorhome, it was even more challenging to not sleep in the same bed. But we maintained our convictions. Debbie slept in the motorhome—and I slept outside in a tent.

Debbie and I were so excited about the *Too Close Too Soon* process and its effect on our lives that we decided to teach a class together at a friend's church. We put together a 4-part course and taught it to the youth group. We shared our journey with the students as a way to inspire them. The graph below is the actual graph of our time together.

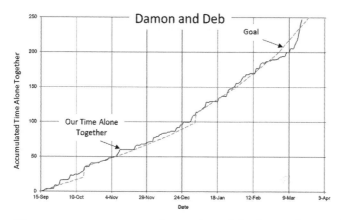

That summer we camped together, fished together, and travelled down the Oregon coast to spend a week camping with Debbie's parents. Our daughters played together while we enjoyed each other's company and spent time with her parents. We were becoming a family.

Debbie and I loved each other deeply. We trusted each other completely and shared our deep Christian faith. We dreamed about a family life together after our devastating divorces. Our relationship was a dream come true for each of us, so it seemed natural for us to begin discussing marriage.

One day I was thinking about our relationship. I hadn't completely shared my history of DV with her and the omission was affecting me. I feared that sharing my dark past would scare her away and I'd lose her. But I loved her too much to keep it a secret. To my surprise, she didn't react when I told her about it. She told me she needed a few days to think about it.

I encouraged her to contact people that knew me and had watched my growth. "Talk to Bob, Steve, Dr. Talley, Don, and Pam," I suggested, "Ask them any question you have." I told her that my main concern was her feeling safe—and that if she wanted to end the relationship I would understand.

Debbie took some time to process my history. Finally, she came back to me and told me she was comfortable with it and that because I'd shared it with her, she trusted me even more. I felt relieved and at peace because I'd disclosed my secrets to her.

In hindsight, maybe this is when our relationship began to decline. Debbie didn't change but I did. I had shared a dark and ugly secret from my past, and I began to fear that she would abandon me.

This revealed itself is subtle ways. We argued a little bit more, we weren't as physically affectionate with each other, and we stopped spending as much time together. We still loved each other and enjoyed being together, but something had changed.

I phoned Debbie to discuss our relationship. I told her I always felt like I was visiting her at her house, and it would be nice for her to come to my house occasionally. Her response triggered some deep pain in me.

"I don't like going to your house, Damon. It's always cold and I'm uncomfortable there," she said.

"Cold", I thought? Just like my house when I was a toddler and my mom and dad were divorcing. Her words invoked the pain of my childhood, making me feel that she was abandoning me, just as I'd experienced as a child.

Tearfully, I shared this chapter of my history with her. Debbie apologized—she didn't know about this part of my past and felt bad for how it had hurt.

Something had changed in our relationship, and we couldn't figure out how to bring back the joy we'd experienced for so much of it.

On Christmas Eve, we sat on the edge of my bed, and I told her I loved her. I told her that she was perfect and that our lives were perfect in almost every way except one. I didn't have custody of Monica, and I couldn't imagine starting a new family with her unless I did. I told her I didn't like these feelings but they were real and I couldn't change them.

The look in her eyes was different than I'd ever seen. Instead of tears, there was anger and hurt. I was pushing her away again, just as I'd done a year earlier.

We spent the holidays trying to figure out how to proceed with our relationship. In early January, we decided to put our relationship at God's feet. If He wanted us to be together, He would have to make a way. After only a few short weeks, Debbie told me she needed a month alone to process her feelings.

On March 3, 2003, we met and jointly decided to end our relationship. I wasn't healthy enough to remarry, and she was fed up with my cycles in our relationship of getting close, followed by distancing.

The most incredible woman I'd ever met was now out of my life. I had been unable to maintain a healthy relationship and I'd pushed her away. Instead of seeking God like I'd done so many times before, I began isolating myself from God.

I found myself fantasizing about the dream of Monica growing up with her biological mom and me again. I thought the dream was dead, but in the pain of losing Debbie, I needed some hope. I repeatedly contacted my ex-wife and spent some time with her. However, each time I saw her I'd leave feeling worse about myself than I did before I saw her. I had no desire to remarry her, but I had a deep desire for

Monica to grow up in a healthy home with her parents.

I continued to distance myself from God and from my friends as well. I was ashamed for allowing myself to drift toward my ex-wife, but I still couldn't let go of my dream. I attended church sporadically, and I stopped tithing regularly, convincing myself that I'd "catch up" on my tithe when I got my annual bonus from Microsoft.

After visiting my ex-wife one summer evening, God got my attention. My behavior was no longer congruent with the man I had worked so hard to become and I needed to change. I called Dr. Talley and talked with him about my situation.

"Damon, you tell me you want to be a man of integrity," he said. "Let me offer an alternate definition of integrity that I think you will like. God doesn't ask us to be perfect, but asks us to confess our sin."

If we confess our sins, he is faithful and just to forgive us our sins and cleanse us from all unrighteousness.
—1 John 1:9

"Damon, integrity is the time span between mess-up and fess-up. Who do you have in your life that you are fessing up to when you mess up?" he asked.

"There is a couple in my church that I've been talking with," I responded.

"Go to them and ask for their help, and when you mess up let them know immediately. This will keep Satan from filling you with shame," he said.

I called the couple the next day, and I confessed my sins to them. I asked for their help, and we signed a ninety-day commitment contract together.

God is so good. He used those ninety days to draw me closer to Him, and He used that couple to teach me about grace and forgiveness.

Dr. Talley later taught me that my goal shouldn't be perfection, but it should be progress. He challenged me to go back in time and look at when I'd slipped. Growth, he told me, was increasing the time span between moral slips. When I graphed this out, I felt an immediate sense of relief. Even though I was failing, I was still growing!

Monica's mom and I took her to her first day of kindergarten together. She had custody of Monica, but I had visitation rights on weekends. I always wanted full custody, but I felt her relationship with her mom was very important, and I knew going to court would be the only way I'd be granted full custody. I didn't want to go to court, as it would only cause strife between her mom and me.

God knew what was best for Monica. God allowed a situation to happen on Monica's first day of kindergarten that I believe was a small miracle. I won't share the details, but I will say that a month later I went to the courthouse and in less than 5 minutes, the judge signed a piece of paper granting me full custody of Monica. God made a way for me to have custody of Monica, and I've had full custody since then.

I now had no excuses. Debbie was my perfect woman, and I still loved her deeply. I had wounded her deeply six months earlier when we broke up. For that reason, I doubted that I deserved her, but God thought otherwise.

I knew she attended church on Sunday evenings, so I decided to sneak in one evening and look for her. I looked around and saw her, but I didn't let her see me. There she was, beautiful, worshiping Jesus with all of her heart with her arms raised high. I was very nervous and decided to sneak out before she could see me.

The next week I did the same. Once again, I saw her. I was afraid that she would be with another man and was shocked that she was alone.

I summoned all my nerve and walked toward her after church ended. In my heart, I knew that she would either be excited to see me or angry and ask me to leave her alone.

Debbie is a godly woman, and she loves Jesus with all of her heart. She radiates beauty through her gentle demeanor and her heart to serve. When she saw me, there wasn't a hint of anger, but rather a gentle look, a wide smile and a soft voice.

"It's good to see you, Damon. How are you?" she asked.

My heart raced, thrilled that she wasn't angry at me. "It's been a rough couple of months, Debbie. Can we set a date to have coffee?" I asked.

"I'd like that, Damon," she replied, smiling radiantly.

A few days later, I picked her up from her Bible study class. It was a beautiful fall day, the type we both love so much. I drove her to a park overlooking Lake Washington and asked her for forgiveness.

I told her how much I loved her and cared for her. I told her that I wasn't going to waste any time. I was serious and I wanted to court her for marriage, if she would let me.

She smiled and said, "It's about time."

Four months later, I took her to Ruth's Chris Steakhouse, the place we'd had our first romantic date. They had butcher paper on the table and crayons. I sketched out the same sketch that I'd done on our first date years earlier at Cucina Cucina. I looked into her eyes and told her she was 1 in a million, my "Six Sigma Girl."

I took a knee and asked her to marry me.

"Yes!" she said, with tears in her eyes.

We rode in a horse-drawn carriage through downtown

Seattle that evening, dreaming about our future. On June 12, 2004, Debbie and I were married. We had remained sexually pure for our entire relationship. I placed a ring on Amanda's hand telling her I promised to be her step-dad, to love her and raise her to be the woman God wanted her to be.

Debbie placed a ring on Monica's hand promising her to be her step-mom, to love her and raise her to be the woman God wanted her to be.

During our wedding reception, I performed the ceremony and Monica's stuffed bunny, Bubbles, and Amanda's stuffed bear, Teddy were married as well.

We were now a family ready to live the dream God had placed in our hearts.

We knew it wouldn't be easy and we had heard that the divorce rate for second marriages with children was nearly fifty percent higher than for marriages with no children. We were committed to each other, but neither us realized just how hard it would be to raise the family of our dreams.

Footnote:

Debbie and I want to say a special "Thank You" to Dr. Talley for his wisdom and guidance through *Too Close Too Soon*. People thought we were crazy, tracking our time together, scoring the quality of our relationship, and not sleeping in the same bed. Today, many of those people are struggling in their marriages or they've divorced. *Too Close Too Soon* built a strong foundation of trust in our relationship, trust in each other, and trust in God.

We have walked 2 different couples through this process, and it did exactly what it was intended to do. One couple decided to end their relationship because they weren't meant for each other, and the other couple is happily married today with children.

As I write this, we are beginning to counsel another couple through the *Too Close Too Soon* process. We are forever grateful for Dr. Talley's wisdom and our obedience in following through.

Questions to Consider

* Do you believe remaining sexually pure before marriage is the right thing to do?
    * Why or why not?
* Is your relationship built on a foundation of trust?
    * What can you change to build more trust?
* Is your relationship struggling?
    * Consider increasing the amount of time alone together and discussing which times you both enjoyed the most.
* How can I help you?
    * You can find more resources and my contact information at **www.paindriveschange.com**.

11
The Pain of a Prodigal Child

He who was seated on the throne said, "I am making
everything new!" Then he said, "Write this down, for these
words are trustworthy and true."
—Revelation 21:5

In her admirable book, *Strong Fathers, Strong Daughters,* Meg Whitman relates that a daughter's relationship with her dad is the single biggest factor in determining how successful a woman will be later in life. When my daughter, Monica, was very young, I was in a men's group focusing on fathering. One of the men in the group said something I will never forget. "I take my daughter on dates very regularly. I use these times to treat her extremely well, showing her how much I love her. When she's older and dating, I want her to compare how well her date is treating her to how well I've treated her on our dates. If it isn't the same or better, she'll know in her heart she deserves better and immediately move on."

After that revelation, I decided to "date" my daughter.

Through the years, we've had some incredible dates together. One evening when Monica was a little girl, we were waiting for a seat at a little Italian restaurant near our home. Monica picked up *Tarzan*, a children's book, and I read it to her. As we ate our "yummy dinner" together, Monica said, "Daddy, this is my favorite restaurant together. Let's call it the 'Tarzan Place.'"

We've shared many meals together at the Tarzan Place,

coloring, talking, and enjoying their Chicken Alfredo. We began calling our dates "special time". I would sit at the table holding her hand and watch her heart tank get filled with her daddy's love.

Before I married Debbie, I spent most of my time with Monica and we developed a very deep and strong relationship. After I married Debbie, Monica was no longer the center of all of my attention. I now had a wife and a step-daughter, replacing most of our one-to-one time with family time. At first, this was very hard for Monica, and she quickly started acting out. Monica was a very strong-willed child, and parenting her put a strain on my relationship with Debbie.

Fortunately for Monica, she visited her mom every week and spent a couple of weekends a month with her.

One day, Monica called me while I was at work. She was crying hysterically and couldn't stop. I asked her to put Debbie on the phone.

"What happened?" I asked Debbie.

"Monica's mom just called her and told her that she was moving to Las Vegas and couldn't see her as often as she had been," Debbie said.

I quickly drove home. Monica was still crying. I grabbed her and hugged her tightly as she continued crying. "I'm sorry, honey. I know how hard this is," I said as I tried to comfort her.

But her tears wouldn't stop. When we put her to bed that night, she cried herself to sleep because she missed her mom so much. God hates divorce, and once again, I was experiencing why it's so. The children of divorce suffer because of their parent's poor choices, and Monica was suffering. There was nothing I could do except hold her and try to comfort her.

Monica's pain began causing her issues at school. Her

teachers regularly called telling us how defiant she was in class. She was in a Christian school but was struggling with her friendships.

One day I received a call from Monica's best friend's parents.

"Damon, we don't want our daughter to see your daughter anymore. She is a bad influence on her," they said.

When I told Monica about the phone call, she was devastated. She was now being abandoned by her best friend and was feeling the same pain as she did when she heard about her mom moving away.

Monica's behavior continued to worsen, and we couldn't do anything to help her. We took her to counseling but it didn't help. We took her to church and encouraged new friendships, but they didn't happen.

As her father, I felt helpless, and I overcompensated. When Debbie and Monica had issues, I began siding with Monica. This isolated Debbie, and she began to feel helpless. Debbie desperately wanted to be a mother figure to Monica, but the tension in their relationship, combined with my mistake of isolating her, put tension on our relationship. Monica would hear us arguing, and she would fear that Debbie and I would eventually divorce.

Monica was nearly ten, and I wanted to make her tenth birthday very special. I bought her a new dress and shoes. We went out to a very nice Italian restaurant, and I told her how much I loved her. I knew she would be entering adolescence, and this would be a dramatic turning point in her life. I wrote her a letter and shared it with her.

My Letter to Monica on Her Tenth Birthday

...Tomorrow is a big day for you, baby girl. You are turning ten. You are going to start growing from a little girl to a young lady. My prayer is that the seeds of Godly character that I've planted in your heart will continue to grow, and in ten years we can go out and have another special dinner. I will be sitting across the table from a beautiful woman of God, the woman I've prayed and dreamed you would be.

I love you, Monica. Thank you for making me the proudest daddy in the whole world!

—Daddy

I was right, things began to change pretty quickly. Monica started spending more time on the computer and her cell phone. Social media was brand new at the time, and I didn't fully understand it. I observed Monica isolating and noticed that she didn't have any friends close to home. She began talking about people and friends that I had never met, saying she'd met them online. Before I knew it, Monica had built up a new social circle and began resisting going to school, saying that "it hurt too much," and she didn't have any friends there.

Monica wrote me a letter at the end of her sixth-grade year, saying she felt like an outcast at the Christian School and begged me to let her go to public school the next year. I knew it was inevitable, and I knew that I couldn't force her to keep going to a Christian school. I prayed often and fervently, hoping that something would change. But nothing changed—things only got worse.

Monica began attending public school in seventh grade. She would ask to spend time with people that we didn't know. I insisted on meeting her friends' parents before she could spend time with them. I met with Monica's school counselor and she told me that Monica was hanging out with the wrong people at school, and her grades were suffering. They recommended that Monica start seeing a counselor.

Unfortunately, counseling didn't help. On February 18, 2011, I got a call from Monica's school that every father dreads. Monica and her friends were high at school after taking Xanax that they'd stolen from her friend's family medicine cabinet. I would need to come talk school officials.

The school suspended Monica for twenty days. She would have to attend drug and alcohol classes before she returned. We attended a class together. I still remember watching a video clip that showed a cat that was stoned on marijuana.

Monica told me afterwards that this video made her curious to try it. I knew the twenty-day suspension hadn't helped. In my gut, I dreaded what was next.

Only a few months later, we discovered that Monica had been seen smoking marijuana with her friends. We got another phone call from the principal, and he recommended that Monica start seeing a specialist to get help.

I called a few treatment centers but quickly convinced myself that Monica didn't have a problem. I couldn't have been more wrong. Only a few weeks later, I discovered that Monica had written a note saying she wanted to commit suicide.

On Monica's last day of seventh grade, she spent the night with some friends at school. The next day, she acted strangely, and she went to her room and slept on and off for nearly 3 days.

When I confronted her on what was wrong, she admitted that she had taken thirteen "Triple C's," a type of cough drop that she had learned would make you high. A few days later at the doctor's office, I learned that Monica could have easily died from this, and that I needed to watch her closely to ensure that she didn't overdose again.

I was at my wit's end. Monica was out of school and spending time with kids that I didn't approve of. We decided to send her to a leadership camp with the local YMCA. Monica spent 2 weeks at Camp Orkilla on the San Juan Islands. I talked with her counselors, and they told me that she wasn't obeying the rules and was spending time with the troubled kids.

Every year, we take a family vacation at Keller Ferry on Lake Roosevelt, a beautiful place without any cell service or Wi-Fi. We use this time to recharge emotionally and re-connect as a family, as well as to set goals for the following year.

I sensed that the next year was going to be very challenging with Monica. Looking back, my decision to start taking care of myself by taking an early-morning walk of twenty minutes every day and a thirty-minute run 3 times a week gave me the emotional strength to carry me through the next 2 years.

I couldn't have been more right. Now in the eighth grade, Monica's situation rapidly deteriorated. We had caught her smoking in her bedroom. We suspected that she was smoking marijuana regularly.

One day, I met her at the door when she came home. I told her to sit at the dinner table and made her open her backpack and take everything out of it.

She pulled a baggie filled with marijuana and a pipe that she had used to smoke it. At the time, marijuana wasn't legal in Washington State. Monica needed a wake-up call, so I decided to call the police. She wasn't in enough pain yet to make her change the actions that were beginning to control her life.

The police came and informed me that they could

do nothing. Possession of marijuana never resulted in a conviction from the court; however, they offered to talk with her. They had a long conversation with her about the dangers of doing drugs, describing marijuana as a gateway drug. Watching Monica during the conversation, I knew there wasn't enough pain to drive her to change.

I was right. Monica was seeing a counselor, and she asked me to attend a counseling session. She asked Monica a series of questions. At the end of the session, the counselor told me that she was concerned that Monica was struggling with addiction and recommended a drug and alcohol assessment.

Finally, the counselor concluded that she could no longer help Monica until Monica decided that she wanted to change.

A few weeks later, I took Monica on a date to discuss the results of the drug and alcohol assessment. Our dates were special times, and I knew we could talk frankly about the results. We discussed the counselor's recommendation that Monica begin attending intensive outpatient treatment, saying that she had 5 of 7 factors indicating that she struggled with addiction.

Monica looked me straight in the eyes with her beautiful brown eyes and said, "Daddy, I'm done with that. I haven't smoked marijuana in more than 3 weeks. You'll see when we get the pee test results back tomorrow."

I smiled with a great sense of relief. She had stopped smoking on her own, and we wouldn't have to proceed with the counselor's recommendation. We continued enjoying our meal together and I felt peace that I had my little girl back. Satan had tried to destroy her but failed.

Be alert and of sober mind. Your enemy the devil prowls around like a roaring lion looking for someone to devour
—1 Peter 5:8

The next day we got the urine test results back, and I was relieved to find they were negative!

Debbie and I discussed that, and we both began feeling suspicious. Something didn't feel right, but we didn't know what. I began snooping around on Monica's social media.

I was stunned at what I saw. Monica had told her friend that it worked, and thanked her for providing a clean sample of pee for her.

How could a fourteen-year-old girl cheat on a urine test?

I called the drug and alcohol assessment counselor and told her what I'd seen. She confirmed that nobody was in the restroom with Monica when she provided the sample, but it was possible that she had cheated the test.

I was filled with anger, and deeply hurt. Only a few days earlier, my precious baby girl had looked me straight in the eyes and lied to me. She had betrayed me during our most special time.

My pain turned to conviction. My little girl had a problem and she needed her daddy more than she ever had. I knew what I must do and wasted no time. God calls fathers to protect their children, and Monica needed my protection.

I scheduled a private appointment with Monica's counselor. She informed me that Monica had consistently lied. Monica was addicted and it was only getting worse. She shared that Monica might not be able to make wise decisions, and if I didn't do something quickly, she might make a foolish decision that could cost Monica her life.

The counselor recommended that Monica begin inpatient treatment.

The next day, I got on the phone and learned that Sundown Ranch had an open bed and that I could bring Monica the next day. That evening, we talked for hours and she admitted she had a problem. She told me she wanted help and was willing to go.

I went to bed in shock. Why was she so willing to go? I was certain that I'd face resistance the next day. But I didn't.

Monica packed her bags, and we left in the car. The 2 hour drive was surprisingly enjoyable. I shared my hopes and dreams for her and told her how hard this was for me. She told me that she wanted to change.

That evening we watched the movie, *Courageous*, which is about a Christian man who loses his daughter in a car accident. This gives him the conviction he needs to be a devoted father and husband to his son and wife. God knew I was making a courageous decision, and He used the movie to help me maintain my conviction.

After the movie, Monica said, "Dad, he reminds me of you."

The next morning, as we drove into Sundown Ranch, I told Monica, "This is the beginning of a new chapter of your life." Monica wasn't the only teen that would be entering the program, there were about a half-dozen other teens with their parents, as well.

Over the next 2 days, Monica underwent a number of assessments and counseling sessions. I went with the other parents to meetings to learn more about the program. That evening, a couple of patients that had been there for a few weeks shared their testimony with parents and incoming patients. They praised the program and said that they felt like they were going to overcome their addictions with tools the program provided them.

We learned the results of Monica's assessments the next day. She was addicted to marijuana and was struggling to make wise decisions when she was with her friends. The counselors recommended the twenty-eight day program. Monica disagreed with them, arguing that she didn't have a problem.

She begged me to take her home, but I held my ground. This was the hardest decision I'd ever made with Monica. I needed God's strength.

The last few days, I'd been hearing the song, "40" by U2, in my head. I never listened closely to the lyrics, but on this day, I turned this song on and turned the volume up loud enough to permeate my soul. Tears began streaming from my face as I realized that this song was based on Psalm 40:1 that God had given me years earlier depicting the story of my life.

I waited patiently for the Lord
He inclined and heard my cry
He brought me up out of the pit
Out of the mire and clay

I will sing, sing a new song
I will sing, sing a new song

How long to sing this song
How long to sing this song
How long, how long, how long
How long, to sing this song

He set my feet upon a rock
And made my footsteps firm
Many will see
Many will see and fear

I will sing, sing a new song
I will sing, sing a new song

I will sing, sing a new song
I will sing, sing a new song

How long to sing this song
How long to sing this song

How long, how long, how long
How long, to sing this song

Pain drives change. God gave me this song exactly when I needed it. Just as He'd lifted my feet out of the slimy pit, He would lift Monica out, too. He would place her feet on a rock and make her footsteps firm. I would sing a new song. The only question was, "How long to sing this song"?

Only God knew, but I trusted Him.

On December 2, 2011, just 2 days before my forty-fourth birthday, I drove home, leaving Monica, allowing His words from this U2 song to bring me peace in the midst of this storm.

I visited Monica the next weekend but cut my visit short. Monica's counselors told me she was being stubborn and was not listening to them. She was not following the rules, and did not acknowledge that she had a problem.

My visit with her only solidified what they were telling me. My optimistic hopes from the previous weekend quickly turned to hopelessness. How much pain would Monica have to feel before she would finally change?

The Christmas season wasn't the same without Monica. Monica still struggled with addiction, and her behavior was extremely challenging, but she was still my baby girl. My heart ached for her, and I found myself in tears most days.

Getting up early in the morning and taking a walk was now a habit, and I used this time to connect with God and replenish my soul. I listened to worship music on my walks, allowing the words to soothe my soul and add to my trust in Him.

One of my favorite songs during this time was from *Casting Crowns* called, *Praise You in the Storm*. I was in the middle of the storm but I raised my hands to the heavens, knowing that He held my little girl in His hands and that He would restore her.

And I'll praise you in this storm
And I will lift my hands
That you are who you are
No matter where I am
And every tear I've cried
You hold in your hand
You never left my side
And though my heart is torn
I will praise you in this storm

I visited Monica on Christmas Eve. We had a very special time together. They were playing our favorite Christmas movie, *The Grinch that Stole Christmas*, with Jim Carey. We sat together laughing and enjoying each other's company.

I hugged her tightly and said, "goodbye", leaving my daughter to be alone on Christmas Day. "This isn't right", I thought to myself on my drive home. But I had no control over the timing, and I had to trust God. The next day, she called me, crying as shared how much she missed being with her family.

I, too, sobbed uncontrollably and told her how proud I was of her and that we'd get through this trial together.

The next week was Monica's last week of treatment. She had grown strong and told me that she was done smoking marijuana.

Her counselors informed me that Monica still would not accept full responsibility for her actions and that she refused to give up the friends that were still using. If she went home, they said, it would only be a matter of time before she would relapse. I knew she wasn't ready to come home, and I knew that I would have to make another difficult, courageous decision.

Through my research, I had discovered a Christian-based program in Arizona that was 3 months long. I wouldn't be allowed to talk with Monica for the first month, except through letters. I felt at peace about sending her to this program, but I feared her reaction.

I decided to tell Monica right before leaving Sundown. I would drive there to pick her up, then we would go home for a few hours to pack her things and see her family. We would then drive to the airport and fly to Arizona, where I'd drop her off.

Monica was furious. I've never seen her spew the profanities that she did that afternoon when I picked her up. I desperately wanted to enjoy our last few hours together and; fortunately, she calmed down enough for us to enjoy our ride home together.

We arrived at home so she could visit with her family for a few hours. When she learned that they had a dress code and that we had bought her new clothes, she was once again furious. She cried and begged me not to go as she hugged her little brother and sister goodbye.

We barely made our flight. That night we enjoyed special time in Arizona together with a great dinner. We both knew what was coming the next day, and neither of us was ready for it. But I knew that if I didn't follow through with this difficult decision, I'd only be delaying the inevitable. Monica was sick and needed to heal. As her father, I needed to provide the environment for her to heal in.

The next day, we arrived at the treatment center where she'd be staying for the next 3 months. It was a nice place in the middle of the desert. I felt God's peace when I arrived. We went into the counselor's office.

"You have ten minutes before you'll have to leave, Damon," the counselor said.

I felt a knot in my throat as I desperately tried to hold back the tears, but Monica needed me to be strong. She desperately begged me not to leave her, promising to change. Tears filled her beautiful brown eyes, and I could see her desperation. Once again, she felt the pain of abandonment that I'd felt so many times in my life. And now she experienced it abundantly in her life.

But this time it was different. Even though she believed I was abandoning her, I wasn't. I was doing this because I loved her. I had to protect her from destroying herself.

"Damon, you need to leave now," the counselor said.

I hugged Monica tighter than I ever have, and looked deeply into her eyes. "I love you, Monica. I'll be praying for you every day and looking forward to when we can see each other again. Get healthy so we never have to do this again."

She waved goodbye as I walked away, just as she had thirteen years ago (almost to the day) when I had separated from her mother, to try to get myself healthy.

As I drove away, I cried out to God, pleading with Him to protect my little girl and make her healthy. I begged for His peace when I made this decision, but I couldn't find it.

The treatment center called and told me that Monica was begging to call me, threatening to run away if she couldn't talk to me.

I asked them what would happen if she ran away.

They said, "When they run they never get far before coming back. You don't have to worry about that."

"Take care of my little girl," I responded with tears in my eyes.

That evening I sat down for dinner and continued praying for God to give me peace about this decision. I opened Facebook on my cell phone to kill the time only to discover that Monica had logged in and forgotten to log out. I browsed through the messages and discovered that she had been chatting with one of her old friends the night before, while I was in bed. "They told me not to contact you but I decided I would anyway. I've only got 3 months here then I'll come back home and we'll continue doing what we were doing before I entered these stupid programs."

Her words to her friend gave me the peace and conviction I'd been praying for. Monica needed to stay.

The next morning, I got up to take a walk in the desert before the sun came up. As I walked over the hill watching the sunrise, God reminded me of His words, and I posted this on Facebook.

Damon Stoddard
January 6, 2012 · Windows Phone · 🌐 ▾

Sunrise in the desert. Meditating on God's promise in revelation "And He who sits on the throne said, "Behold, I am making all things new." And He *said, "Write, for these words are faithful and true." .

👍 Like   💬 Comment   ↗ Share

I was now entrusting my little girl to Him, and He was preparing to fulfill His promise to make all things new. Unfortunately, Monica would have to stumble her way through her own desert and experience even greater levels of pain before God could fulfill His promise.

Have you ever been separated from your child for more than a few days without the ability to communicate with her directly? One of the requirements of this program was that I couldn't talk with Monica for the first month. I could write her letters, but I couldn't talk with her. I thought of her from the moment I woke up in the morning until the time I fell asleep at night. I prayed for her emotional healing and I prayed that Jesus would fill her heart with His love.

My inability to communicate directly with Monica deepened my prayer life and reliance on God. I had no control. I had to trust Him with my little girl. I knew her pain because I'd experienced the pain of being separated from my parents when I was a child.

I wanted desperately to remove her pain but I couldn't. But I also knew that *pain drives change*. My prayer was that her pain would be great enough to change her heart without breaking her will. My morning walks listening to worship music provided me the peace that I needed to make it through this season. God continued to remind me that He would make all things new.

I also found solace and courage in one of my favorite books, *Strong Fathers, Strong Daughters*. I listened to this audiobook while running on the treadmill. The author's words reminded me that, if I could stay strong in this season of life, it would change the rest of her life. Her stories gave me the hope that I needed to push through.

Our first conversation was short and filled with tears. Monica was very depressed and wanted desperately to come home.

"It'll be okay," I told her. "Use this time to grow closer to Jesus and heal from all of the pain you have experienced in life." We said "goodbye", and I reminded her I'll be visiting in a month.

I arrived in Arizona a day early. I hadn't seen my little girl in more than 2 months! I drove by the place she was staying, hoping to get a glimpse of her, knowing that if I did I wouldn't be able to stop.

I barely slept that night and got up early in the morning so that I wouldn't be late. I sat in their waiting room anxiously waiting to see her. She walked in and when she saw me, her smile was bigger than any I'd ever seen. She ran toward me and hugged me tighter than she had ever hugged me. Her hug reminded me of our hug the first time I'd disciplined her in the motorhome. We were reunited, and our hearts were filled with joy.

The next 2 days together were the best time we've ever spent together. Monica was different. Her anger and bitterness was replaced with gentleness and peace. Her scowl was replaced with a smile, and her pain was replaced with joy. This picture was taken that weekend. Her smile and embrace capture the essence of her heart.

Just as He promised a few months earlier, He had made her new!

We enjoyed our special time together over a great meal. Monica began weeping with guilt. On her previous birthday, she told me she was stoned and had mocked our most precious time together. She asked my forgiveness and told me she never wanted to go back to being that person.

Monica invited me to her church that evening. My eyes were filled with tears as we worshiped together. Satan tried to steal my little girl but had failed. I had my little girl back!

Monica came home on Easter weekend. We spent the morning at church and had dinner together that afternoon. My heart was full of joy as I watched Monica hunt Easter eggs with her brother and sisters. Our family was together and we loved each other deeply. We'd weathered the storm of addiction and were ready to start the next chapter of our lives.

But addiction had not finished its work with my daughter. Within a few weeks, she began sneaking around and disobeying the rules. She began spending time with her old friends that I'd explicitly told her she couldn't see. The beauty and peace I'd seen only a few months earlier was replaced with anger and rebellion.

On her last day of school, Monica asked to spend the weekend with her friends. When I told her that she couldn't see them, she refused to listen and ran away from home.

After only a few days with her friends, she contacted me and told me she wouldn't be coming home; she wanted to live with her mom for the summer.

Monica only contacted me a few times that summer from her mom's, and every conversation turned into an argument. I visited her late in the summer and gave her the choice to move home for her tenth-grade school year and to follow my rules or live with her mom.

A few weeks later, Monica's mom called me from a gas station down the street. Monica wasn't following her rules and wouldn't be living with her anymore.

The next year was the most challenging year as a parent I've ever faced. Monica refused to obey my rules and often ran away to spend time with her friends. When she was at home, she refused to get up for school and began failing most of her classes. She was regularly smoking pot again. And again, I was at my wit's end.

But things only got harder. Monica ran away on Thanksgiving. I had discovered where she was staying and I contacted the police. They picked her up, and she rode in the back of the police car to meet me. Unfortunately, this didn't change her actions; it only made her angrier.

She ran away again and was gone for nearly a week. I didn't know where she was, and I worried about her safety. She was spending time with people that were much older than she was and putting herself in situations that could have easily harmed her.

I discovered that she was going to a rave that evening. Deeply concerned, I called my best friend and my brother and asked them to help me find Monica. It would not be easy because a rave can have hundreds, even thousands, of kids, but she was my daughter and I needed to find her to protect her.

We prayed and asked God to help us find her. We contacted the police that were near the rave and asked for their help as well, giving them a picture of Monica.

I dropped my brother off and he began walking through the crowd. A few minutes later my cell phone rang. "I've got her," he said.

Monica looked terrible and was stoned. She was filled with anger and began spewing venom through her words at me, "I hate you."

"That's okay, Monica," I replied. "I love you and I won't let you kill yourself. Get in the truck."

My brother had to sit with her to keep her from jumping out of the door, but eventually we got her home.

I knew she wouldn't stay at home and I needed help. In Washington State, there is a law that helps parents with out-of-control teens. If I could get a judge to grant me an At Risk Youth Petition, she would be required by law to abide by my rules. Violation of these rules could result in spending time in juvenile detention.

The judge granted me the petition. Monica was now required by law to attend intensive outpatient treatment for her addictions. She was required to go to school and follow my rules.

But Monica still wouldn't follow my rules, and she

wouldn't go to school without a fight. One morning, I had to carry her down the stairs. She spit in my face. "I hate you!" she shouted.

"I love you, Monica, and I won't allow you to destroy yourself."

She was now spending time with new friends from her intensive outpatient center. One evening, she didn't come home on time but asked me to come pick her up. I waited in my car for an hour, until she finally showed up in the parking lot. Her behavior was odd. I later discovered she had speedballed with these friends.

Speedballing is a term used to describe the use of meth and heroin to get high. Monica had never tried hard drugs, and she was now on a path that could easily take her life, so I requested a court hearing.

Monica sat on one side with her attorney while I sat on the other side. I pleaded with the judge to help, and the judge recommended we separate for at least ninety days to protect our long-term relationship. She told Monica that if she didn't follow the rules, she'd find herself in juvenile detention.

Afterwards, I asked Monica to get into my car, but once again, she refused. I reminded her that if she chose to run away she was choosing her consequences.

She told me that she'd rather be in juvenile than living in my home.

I told her that I loved her and said goodbye.

The police found Monica on Friday of that week. She'd been sleeping on her friends' couches. She spent the weekend in juvenile detention. I picked her up on Monday after the judge told her she'd be on house arrest for a week.

Monica came home for a week with an ankle bracelet. She was only allowed to go to school in the morning and attend her intensive outpatient classes. On the drive home, she told me how disgusting her weekend was in juvenile and she never wanted to go back.

Things didn't get better at home. Monica visited her mom for Mother's Day and called me telling me she wouldn't be coming home; she was going to live with her mom.

Pain drives change. Monica was destroying herself with her actions, and it was beginning to affect the rest of the family. In the process, Monica's problems became my problems. I carried the burden of her disobedience on my shoulders. I was angry and my heart was hardening towards her.

It was now easier for me to let my daughter go than it was to have her continue living in my home.

I talked to my men's group and I asked them for their advice.

"Damon, she is your prodigal child. You need to let her go. God loves her more than you do; you'll need to trust Him for her future."

I wrestled with their words and read the scripture multiple times every day. Pain had driven a change in the prodigal son's heart. The father didn't pursue him but waited patiently on his porch for his son to "come to his senses."

I began praying fervently that God would "bring Monica to her senses." I asked everyone I knew to pray the same thing.

Slowly God's peace began to lift my heart. Monica was nearly sixteen, and I had invested my whole life in her. She had watched me overcome many trials in life and had seen God's hand at work. I had tried to fill her with every bit of wisdom I knew, disciplined in love, and allowed her to stumble and learn from her mistakes. I'd set firm boundaries and I'd protected her.

Finally, one day I woke up with a renewed sense of peace. "Monica's problems are Monica's problems. I'm going to stop trying to fix her and allow the natural consequences of life teach her life's lessons," I thought.

I remembered a sermon from years ago, encouraging parents to invest in their relationships with their teens. I decided that my goal with Monica was to deepen our relationship and be "safe" for her to open up with and share her struggles. I would no longer try to "fix her." Rather, I would allow life's challenges to teach her. I would be there when she stumbled, I would encourage her along the way—but I would no longer carry the burden of her problems.

I spent Father's Day with Monica. As I was driving her back to her mom's, she noticed that I was crying. I told her how much I loved her and that I had made a decision: She was free to choose where she wanted to live. I, of course, wanted her to live with me, but if she decided to live with her mom, I would support that and I would continue loving her.

I hugged her and said,"goodbye", entrusting my little girl to Him.

Something changed in Monica between saying goodbye on Father's Day and hello in early August on our annual camping trip to Lake Roosevelt. For the first time since she was a little girl, Monica *wanted* to camp with her family.

She spent the days with us just relaxing and enjoying each other's company. She was more respectful to Debbie, and she was more open with me. She spent time talking with my dad. She laughed. She played in the sun.

Monica's time away had helped her realize that her family loved her deeply, and Monica had missed us deeply. I drove her to her mom's house and said goodbye, reminding her once again that I loved her and that, while she could decide where she would live, she had to decide before school started in a few weeks.

Monica decided to come back home a few weeks later. We welcomed her with open arms and celebrated her return. A few months earlier, she continually ran away from her family—and now she was running towards us.

Monica began following the rules without arguing. She changed her circle of friends and began going to school every day.

We began spending special time together again on our date nights. Our conversations were deeper and more meaningful than they'd ever been, and she began sharing intimate details of her life, trusting me to guide her. Monica was allowing me to be a father. I was now emotionally safe, allowing her to trust me.

I asked Monica to share a little bit of her story in hopes that it will help those are struggling with addiction or have a child that is struggling with addiction.

Monica's Letter

The trials I experienced but never understood as a child shaped me into a person unrecognizable from who I am today, and I'm sure indistinguishable from who I will be in the future. When I tell some people that I was addicted to pills by the age of thirteen years old, they shudder, or brush it off as fiction. But that is who I was; that's who I became by watching the people who raised me fall. When I tell some people I started huffing at age eleven or cutting myself, they are in disbelief. But that is who I became as a product of watching the people who raised me disappear.

A time came about in my life in which I was addicted to pain medication, scouring for half-smoked cigarettes in the streets, and going to intensive outpatient. I was in junior high, but I never went to school. Fifteen years old, I was doing drugs, but in a program meant to keep me from doing drugs. Rebelling against the only people who cared enough, and truly tried to better me. I was choosing false love and immediate comfort and validation over true, unconditional love over myself. This isn't to say my home life was perfect-in my personal opinion it was anything but. I felt a disconnect with my family and myself.

In trying to write this I had many conversations with my dad. He asked me quite a few times, 'Did you do drugs to numb the pain? To not feel sad?' And though I am positive that that is true for some, most, many drug addicts/alcoholics-that is not true for me. I did drugs because I felt a disconnect with everything and everyone around me-an absence of feeling.

I read a quote that has forever impacted me. 'Professor Peter Cohen argues that human beings have a deep need to bond and form connections; it's how we get our satisfaction. If we cannot connect to each other, we will connect with anything we can find-the whirr of a Roulette Wheel or the prick of a syringe. He says we should stop talking about addiction all together and, instead, call it 'bonding.' A heroin addict has bonded with heroin because she couldn't bond fully with anything else. So the opposite of addiction is not sobriety, it is human connection.'

I think the moment I decided to clean myself up was when I attended AA meetings with my dad at church. He went for his own stuff and was so serious about it. I went as a way to spend time with him. I decided I was going to live with my mom because something didn't work where I was. While living with her over the summer, I experienced how it would feel to continue down the path I was living. I had experienced it before but never at that magnitude. Something opened my heart up prominently that summer.

Mother's Day 2016 will be my 3 years clean date. Eighteen years old, clean 3 years, that's nuts! After a year-long adjustment period I'm back to normal (or I'm normal for me).

—*Monica*

A few weeks ago, we celebrated Monica's eighteenth birthday over an incredible meal. She hasn't touched a drug since the day she decided to live with her mom two and a half years earlier. My little girl was now a young woman, and I wrote her a letter telling her how proud I was of the woman she'd become by overcoming adversity after adversity.

"I'm fortunate to have been misfortunate," Monica had told me a few weeks earlier over lunch.

Her words helped convict me to write the book you are now reading.

I love you, Monica!

—*Daddy*

Questions to Consider

- If you have a daughter, do you "date" her?
  - Why or why not?
- If your child were struggling with addiction would they feel safe enough to tell you?
  - What can you change to build more trust?
- What do you do to spend "special time" with your children?
  - How do you know this time is truly "special" to them?
- If you have a child struggling with addiction what is the courageous decision you need to make?
  - Why haven't you made this decision?
- How can I help you?
  - You can find more resources and my contact information at **www.paindriveschange.com**.

12
The Joy of Family

See, I am setting before you today a blessing and a curse—the blessing if you obey the commands of the Lord your God that I am giving you today; the curse if you disobey the commands of the Lord your God and turn away from the way that I command you today by following other gods, which you have not known.
—Deuteronomy 11:26-28

Through writing this book, I've realized how incredibly blessed my life is today. Nearly seventeen years ago, I sat in front of my video camera describing my feelings. I had lost all hope that I'd ever have the life and family I so desperately longed for. I came to a fork in the road and I had a tough decision to make—would I take the easy path to avoid the intense pain I was feeling or would I take the hard path and let the pain transform me into the man God designed me to be?

I chose the hard path. In the process, God taught me how to find joy in my pain. Ironically, this book came about because Microsoft laid me off after 12.5 years of faithful service. For many people, the pain of losing their job creates anger and bitterness toward their employer. I chose to find joy in the pain of my layoff. With a heart full of gratitude, I wrote a simple letter and posted it to my blog:

"Thank you Microsoft and Goodbye."

Choosing joy seems to have resonated with those who read my blog. It went viral! Nearly 30,000 people read it and commented on it. Many of those who read my blog encouraged me to write a book and use it to motivate people.

A month and a half after my layoff, I was seeking direction and I met with Greg, a mentor and friend who has watched God's hand transform me. The last time we met, Greg recommended I write a book, but I didn't follow through. He told me that God had given me a gift with my time off from work and that I should use it wisely. He told me he'd written a book and inspired me to write the book you are now reading.

Ironically, I recently accepted a new job at Microsoft, 5 months after I was laid off. God wanted me to write this book and He made a way!

I want to end my book leaving you with hope. I don't know what your situation is, but I believe you picked this book up because you are in pain. You are facing a fork in the road and you have a decision to make. Make the hard decision: Choose obedience.

I chose obedience, and He fulfilled His promise to bless me.

Debbie and I knew that the odds were stacked against us when we each brought a child into our second marriage. We took a step-parenting class, and I recall a statistic that the divorce rate is 50% higher when second marriages have children versus when they don't. My research indicates that the divorce rate for second marriages with children is between 65% and 75%.

But we both knew that God put us together for a purpose, so we decided to beat those odds and build the family we both dreamed about. We're beating the odds, after eleven and one-half years of marriage, we love each other more than we ever. We have 4 children—Amanda, Debbie's daughter, is now twenty-one, Monica is my daughter and is now eighteen, Noelle is our daughter and is now 9, and Nathan is our son and he is now 7. When people see us together, they would never guess that we are a blended family.

As I mentioned in an earlier chapter, Debbie and I made a commitment not only to each other but also to our children on the day we were married.

Debbie felt it was very important for us to move out of our own homes and into a different home when we were married. We found a house that was less than 2 miles from where Debbie grew up and where her parents still lived. Our first meal together at our new home was at our rehearsal dinner. A close friend cooked an incredible dinner, and we invited our closest friends to join us. We asked our pastor, Don, to bless our home that evening.

We packed our belongings before we left on our honeymoon. While we were gone, a moving company carted everything to a new house. Returning from our honeymoon, we settled in to a new home and a new family.

Debbie was a full-time nurse before we were married. When we started married life together, she decided to work only one day a week to concentrate on raising our family. This was a difficult decision, but we knew that her sacrifice was congruent with our goal of raising a healthy family.

Debbie brought structure to my life at home. Before we were married, Monica and I ate meals when we were hungry, mostly frozen food or fast food. This changed after we were married: we had a home-cooked meal at 6:00 every night and enjoyed dinner at the dinner table. We've maintained this habit of eating dinner together since the day we were married. I'm certain this habit strengthened our family.

Studies suggest that having dinner together as a family at least 4 times a week has positive effects on child development. Other tangible benefits of family dinners are reduced risk of obesity, substance abuse, eating disorders, and an increased chance of graduating from high school.

While doing research for one of his books about the factors which contribute to healthy and effective families, Dr. Gary Smalley learned that he could find quite a bit of advice on what NOT to do—but he could find only a few hints about what TO do.

He did discover that healthy families go camping together. While that may seem odd at first, it makes good sense. I'll bet that some of your strongest memories as a child include camping trips with your family.

Fortunately, it was easy for us to camp together—I had a motorhome! We began camping regularly even when we were dating and continued camping together after we were married. We have camped on the Pacific Ocean, Puget Sound, Lake Crescent, the North Cascades, Lake Roosevelt, my dad's backyard, Fish Lake, and the San Juan Islands. That motorhome that I had once lived in has provided some incredible family memories.

One fall, we decided to camp at the North Cascades for Debbie's birthday. Right before pulling out of town, we got a flat tire and had to get it fixed. As we were driving up the North Cascades highway, the door blew off. I was able to re-attach it, and we continued up the road. It was cold, and I planned to build a roaring fire to keep us warm—but I forgot to bring some firewood.

I saw firewood for sale on the side of the road but couldn't slowdown in time, so I had to turn the motorhome around. In the process of turning around, we got stuck in a ditch. Now I was blocking half of the North Cascades highway!

As Debbie and the kids sat there, totally embarrassed, I waved cars through, praying for a tow truck to come. Finally, a family with a big 4-wheel drive truck stopped and pulled us out.

We laughed and laughed and laughed as we drove to our camp spot.

That night, we enjoyed the warm fire and cozied up in the motorhome for a nice, warm night's sleep—or so we thought.

We woke up in the middle of the night to the sound of mice feet walking across the tin foil on the brownies Debbie had made. A mouse had eaten a hole in the top and stuffed itself on our brownies.

After going back to sleep, I woke up again. This time because I was freezing. The battery had died and the furnace had stopped working. I had to start the motorhome so that I had enough battery power to start the generator to run the furnace. I continued doing this every hour all night long to keep my family warm.

None of us got much sleep that night, but we had an incredible weekend together—riding bikes, hiking, and enjoying the majestic beauty.

The gas gauge on the motorhome didn't work, but I was certain we had enough gas to make it home, so I didn't stop to fill it up. I was wrong. The motorhome ran out of gas about a quarter-mile from the gas station. I walked to the station, borrowed a gas can, and put enough gas in the motorhome to drive it to the gas station.

As we drove home, we laughed and laughed and laughed.

On the surface, it might seem like this trip was a catastrophe. But the truth is the exact opposite. We were together as a family the whole weekend, without anything to do but spend time together. It was ten years ago and I can remember it like it was yesterday! Even today, if I bring up that trip, we all start laughing and laughing—and laughing!

My dad lives about 6 hours away in a house that is too small to accommodate my family when we visit. He invited us over but we resisted. Finally, God convicted me that I needed to honor my father, so we drove the motorhome to his house and camped in his back yard.

Dad took the kids out to gather eggs from the chickens, and he made breakfast for us with his Dutch oven. We went biking together and had ice cream, we watched movies and swam in Lake Roosevelt, where I'd swam as a kid. We picked huckleberries and went wading in the creek. We lit fireworks and watched the beautiful sunset. We listened to *The Carpenters* and relaxed in the warm sun. Dad was enjoying his grandkids and they were enjoying him.

We've continued this tradition nearly every year since. In fact, the highlight of our summers is camping in Grandpa's back yard.

After our first trip to his house, I decided to show Debbie and my new family where my mom had grown up. We took the ferry that my grandpa had piloted for 37 years across Lake Roosevelt to the little town of Keller Ferry. It was more beautiful than I remembered and I told Debbie I wanted to come back later that summer for a weeklong camping trip.

A few weeks later, we packed the motorhome and the boat, and then we drove back to Keller Ferry. During the drive, we roasted for 5 hours in the blazing sun—without air conditioning to keep us cool.

That week we had the best camping trip of our lives, so we decided to camp there every summer. We boated and biked, swam and roasted marshmallows. We caught crawdads and built sandcastles. We jumped off cliffs and took sunset cruises on my boat. We asked my grandpa to tell us stories and videotaped him as we learned that he had dug out the marina with a steam-powered bulldozer.

We learned that he had helped plant the trees that provided our shade. My grandpa created a spot where generations of his bloodline would come to enjoy each other and build memories for a lifetime. We camp there every year with our best friends and their children, as well as my dad and other members of my extended family.

Keller Ferry has become a cornerstone of our family. I believe it was a gift from God because I chose to honor my father that year by visiting him in his home with my family.

A few weeks ago, a tree fell on the motorhome and punctured the roof, causing it to leak. I couldn't sell it because it was so old and tired, so I called a wrecking yard. They told me it would cost me $500 to have them crush it. I didn't have the heart to crush it, so I posted it on Craigslist.

I received a call the next day from a man who said he was interested. His wife had cancer and they were staying in a motel. That night was their last night, and they didn't have any place to live. He was a contractor and had the skills to fix the motorhome, so we gave it to him. My kids cleaned and vacuumed it with him, their hearts filled with joy. The motorhome I'd once lived in when I didn't have a home was now a home for another family in need.

Debbie and I both wanted children of our own, but she didn't think we'd be able to. She had struggled with infertility in her first marriage. Amanda was their only child, even though she wanted more. I told Debbie not to worry about it, I trusted God. If He wanted us to have children then we would. I told her either way was fine with me.

It didn't take long. After being married less than a year, I came home from work and Debbie gave me a surprise gift. I unwrapped it to find a baby bottle! We were going to have a baby! We discovered that she was a girl and was due near Christmas.

Our little girl was born on December 30, 2005. Just as Jesus was a gift from God and was born on Christmas, our baby was a gift from God, so we named her Noelle.

Debbie and I both started having dreams that we would have a son. She felt like we should call him Nathan, and I wanted his middle name to be Dean after my deceased brother.

On March 7, 2008, my only son, Nathan, was born. We now were a family of 4. We both wanted more children but felt like we were too old, so Debbie was "snipped" after her C-section.

Children are a gift from the LORD;
they are a reward from him.
—Psalm 127:3

Our new children dramatically changed our family dynamics. Our attention was now focused on the younger children; unfortunately, in so doing, our relationships with our older girls suffered. Amanda was now a teenager and began spending more time with her friends. Where we had once enjoyed dinner as a family nearly every night, we now were only together a few times a week. Monica, too, was entering adolescence and experiencing the struggles that I mentioned in the previous chapter.

Debbie and I knew we had to do something to keep us all from drifting apart. When the older girls were younger, we would rent a motel room with a swimming pool and stay the night as a way of getting away alone together. We decided we'd do it again. Nathan and Noelle were so excited that they packed their own suitcases! Noelle was only 5, but even then, she revealed her servant's heart by helping her little brother pack his suitcase.

We jumped in the car and took off for the "Show and Tell" (when we said we were going to a hotel Nathan heard us say "show and tell," so that's what he called it).

We stopped and had breakfast together. I don't know what it is, but our family loves to eat out at restaurants together. When we arrived at the motel, we put on our bathing suits and jumped in the pool. The older girls jumped into the hot tub while I played with the little ones in the wading pool.

We enjoyed dinner together at Kyoto, a Japanese Steakhouse. We rented a separate room for the older girls and after we put the little ones to bed, we snuggled with them eating junk food and watching movies. We were gone for less than 24 hours, but it brought us together as a family.

On my drive home I asked myself, "Why don't we do this more?" We all loved it and it only cost us a couple of hundred dollars. I had an epiphany—our lives were becoming so busy that we neglected to schedule time to be alone together as a family. Years earlier, I heard something I'll never forget: If you want to know what is important to somebody, just look at where they spend their time and money.

Even though I said my family was everything to me, my calendar didn't show it. Our older girls were growing up, and if I didn't change something, they'd be grown and gone—and I would regret not having spent more time with them.

I began praying about how I could proactively schedule family time before scheduling anything else. That Christmas, we surprised the older girls by telling them we'd be going to San Diego on a family vacation. Their eyes lit up and they giggled like little kids. "We're going to California...we're going to Disneyland!"

Seattle is cold and rainy in January; the sun rarely appears. We needed some sunshine, so we packed our things and flew away to the sun to spend a week together. I rented a car and we headed to our condo, but first we needed to stop at In-N-Out Burger!

Our condominium was right on the beach. We unloaded the car and headed out to play in the waves and sand. As we watched the sunset from our balcony, Debbie and I looked at each other and realized that the money we were spending on this vacation was an investment in our family relationships.

That week was a blast! We visited Disneyland, Sea World, the San Diego Zoo Safari, and we frolicked in the pool like dolphins. We walked on the beach and built sandcastles. We ate tasty junk food and drew closer to one another. Before our trip was over, everyone started asking when we could go back!

We've returned to San Diego twice since then. I've made a decision that we will take a trip to the sun every other winter as a family, even if the older girls can't make it.

A few months ago, during family dinner, I said with a stern look on my face, "Girls, I have something to tell you."

They looked at me as if something was wrong. "We're going to Mexico this winter!" I said with a smile on my face. They jumped around excitedly, just as if they did a few years earlier when we told them we were going to California.

Family vacations have always drawn us closer together. A few years ago, we learned that Debbie had cancer. By the grace of God, after only a few months of treatment, she was cancer-free.

We flew to San Diego as a family and had the best family vacation ever. Debbie and I rejoiced because Amanda, now an adult, and Monica, now a teenager, still wanted to spend time with the family.

My epiphany made me realize that I needed to be more proactive about scheduling my time away with my kids and my wife. Instead of giving my loved ones my "left-over" time, I needed to give them my best time. I thought about how I could make this time away "automatic." I realized that a timeshare condo would be perfect. My time would be automatically scheduled—because I'd have to pay for the condo whether I used it or not.

On a whim, I pulled up Craigslist and searched for timeshare condominiums on Lake Chelan. I had a faint memory of a place and decided to check prices. To my surprise, I discovered a condo that someone was giving away!

I quickly called them up, and a few weeks later, we owned a condo in Manson with a view of Lake Chelan. We could use it for 3 weeks of the year, and it would cost us around $2,200 per year.

When we pulled in to see our condo for the first time, we were overwhelmed with joy. The Eastern Washington sun was warm enough to allow us to swim in the swimming pools and Lake Chelan. The sliding glass door of our condo opened up to a large grassy area with a view of the sunrise and sunset on the lake. We boated and biked, swam and ate. We relaxed and talked. The older girls went out and found frogs (just like they did at Keller Ferry). We were only there for 4 days, but we once again bonded as a family.

I later discovered that by subleasing our condo in the summer, I could almost pay the entire year's dues! We now had a place to go and bond as a family and it was nearly free!

Our next allotted time to stay at the condo came at an inconvenient time, so we tried to talk ourselves out of going. I refused the temptation and pushed through the barriers that were keeping us from going. We spent an incredible weekend together with our little kids. If we hadn't had the condo, we wouldn't have gone on this vacation!

After returning to our home, I asked Debbie if she wanted to go back for our remaining few days of time to celebrate her birthday. She thought it would be nice for us to be together without the children but felt selfish for wanting to go.

I convinced her to go, and we spent the evening together celebrating her birthday without the children. Our time alone drew us closer than we'd been in months. During that time, we fell back in love with each other and with the area, so decided we'd like to own a house there.

We spent the next morning looking for houses and soon realized we couldn't afford to live there. We met a couple and they overheard us talking about our desire to own a home in Manson. They were building condos and were looking for an investment partner.

One year later, we broke ground and today we co-own a property with 8 condos, an infinity edge pool, and a hot tub overlooking Lake Chelan.

Today, we try to get away at least once a month as a family to stay there. I believe God blessed us with this property because of our obedience in investing in our marriage by choosing to invest in our relationship by celebrating Debbie's birthday together.

Years earlier, Dr. Talley taught us that the quality of our relationship was directly proportional to the amount of accumulated time spent alone together. Our experiences with family vacations and getaways have validated his hypothesis. Our time together as a couple and as a family have strengthened our relationships more than anything else we've done.

We've built routines into our lives to intentionally spend time away alone together. As I mentioned earlier, we camp on Lake Roosevelt every year, and we vacation in the sun every other year during the winter. We camp in my dad's backyard every Fourth of July. We stay at our condo in Manson 1 or 2 times a year (during the off season), and we try to get away at least one weekend per month with our younger children.

We recently bought a travel trailer and plan to take camping trips on a regular basis. Debbie and I also prioritize our time together. We get away for a weekend 2 to 3 times a year—always on her birthday, our anniversary, and another time around Valentine's Day. We also have a date night at least once a month. As you can see, our calendar definitely reflects our priorities.

When I was attending counseling with Pam, she recommended a book that I'd strongly recommend, *An Elephant in the Living Room, A Leader's Guide for Helping Children of Alcoholics*. The book referenced a study by Drs. Steven Wolin and Linda Bennett about family rituals. Family rituals are ways of sharing meaning and identity. These rituals are the traditions that celebrate events in the life of family—birthdays, holidays, weekends, dinnertime, and so on.

Their research found that families with alcoholism who protected family rituals were least likely to produce children that would grow up to be alcoholics. Furthermore, they discovered that the greater the change in family rituals during the time of heaviest parental drinking, the more likely would be the recurrence of alcoholism in the children's generation. Reading this made an indelible impression on me; I took out a red sharpie pen and wrote: ***Family Rituals***.

God knew what I needed when I married Debbie. She had grown up in a family that had strong family rituals. She has carried those same traditions into our family.

As I mentioned earlier, we have dinner together almost every night as a family. Birthdays are special occasions, as well. Debbie always cooks our children's favorite meal and makes birthday cake. We invite our extended families, and now that the girls are older, their boyfriends, too.

After dinner, we edify our children. We go around the table and each person shares what they love about the person who has the birthday. It is amazing to watch how touching this exercise is to the recipient. Finally, we sing Happy Birthday, open presents, and eat cake.

I'm certain most people reading this have similar rituals. I encourage you to keep these rituals going, especially when there is a crisis in your family.

We also have strong rituals for Thanksgiving and Christmas. We celebrate Thanksgiving, like most families, with a large meal. My mom used to make rolls using large tuna fish cans and handed this tradition to our family. We gorge ourselves on these rolls! We enjoy family, pie, and football.

Our Christmas season starts with our whole family going out to find and cut a Christmas Tree, followed by putting up the Christmas lights on our home while listening to *Jars of Clay Christmas.* We get family pictures with Santa, and we all sit down to watch *Home Alone,* Debbie's favorite Christmas show, while laughing hysterically.

On Christmas Eve, we have dinner with Debbie's parents, followed by church services at their church as a family. On Christmas morning, I get up and turn on the gas fireplace to warm up the living room and play *Carpenters' Christmas* on the stereo. I open the pocket doors into the living room, and the kids come in to see the gifts that Santa brought them.

Debbie makes the same meal every Christmas morning: a breakfast casserole, orange slices with powdered sugar, and homemade cinnamon rolls. One year, she forgot the ingredients for the casserole and had to make a different kind of casserole. The kids were practically in tears because "we always eat that."

Once again, I'm certain that most reading this have special traditions for Thanksgiving and Christmas. My encouragement to you is to be consistent. Keep these rituals going!

We have similar rituals for Easter, and I already mentioned we visit my dad every year on the Fourth of July.

We also have daily rituals with the children while they are young. After brushing their teeth and putting on their pajamas, they snuggle in bed, but not before putting their feet out so that I can tear their socks off. (For some reason they giggle after I tear their socks from their feet.) I then read a devotional to them. We hold hands, and each child prays, starting with what they are thankful for. When everyone has prayed, I say a final prayer, give the kids a hug and a kiss, then Debbie sings them a couple of Christian songs.

When Debbie isn't home I sing to the kids. (I have an awful singing voice, but the kids always tell me I'm a good singer.) As I sing, Noelle sings with me, just like her mom sings to her and it softens my heart. Finally, I sing a silly song to them and they laugh and laugh.

Fathers, if you have little kids at home, I strongly encourage you to create a daily ritual like ours. Some nights when it is very late, we choose not to read the devotional, but our kids beg us to do so. These rituals fill their hearts with our love and Christ's love every night before they go to sleep.

A few years ago, I built a daily ritual calendar. I'll be honest; I haven't been as consistent as I'd like on these daily rituals but I try.

Mom Mondays—We bring ice cream to my mom and visit her.

Tickle Tuesdays—I tickle the kids, rolling around on the floor.

Whatever Wednesdays—We do whatever we want.

Thankful Thursdays—We spend the evening with friends that also homeschool.

Family Friday—We spend time with one another playing games, riding bikes, etc.

Slow Saturdays—We leave Saturdays open to do whatever we want.

Sabbath Sundays—We go to church and relax for the rest of the day.

Amanda graduated from a Christian school and Monica attended a Christian school through sixth grade. In both instances, we saw the profound affect that friends had on our teenage children. I'm a strong believer in the power of positive relationships and try to surround myself with people whom I can learn and grow from and who will hold me accountable to being the man I want to be.

We want our kids to live Christ-centered lives when they grow up, so we surround them with other children with similar beliefs. Our closest friends have a daughter the same age as Noelle and a son the same age as Nathan. They love each other deeply and are best friends as well. A few years ago, we invited them to join us for our annual Keller Ferry camping trip. They loved it so much that now they come back every year. We also invited them to stay with us in the springtime at our condo. They loved that so much that they come back every year as well.

The same Christian school I mentioned above has a Christ-centered football program. I enrolled Nathan when he was 6 and began coaching. This year, I'm the head coach for his football program. There are at least forty other dads coaching their sons on the various teams through eighth grade. I'd never seen so many dads volunteer at church.

I believe this program is one of the most significant things I can do to raise Nathan up to be a godly man of character. He's surrounded by godly men, godly children, and godly character development through football. I believe this program is a "man-making machine," and I'm thankful that I could be a part of it.

When Noelle was reaching school age, Debbie and I began praying about homeschooling. I found a book called *Disciple Like Jesus for Parents.* The author provided the shocking facts that 75% to 90% of our young people just walk away from church upon graduating from high school.

If our goal was to raise children that centered their lives on Christ, the odds were against us. Going to church wouldn't be enough, and raising them in a Christian school wouldn't be enough either. The author stated that the average Christian home spends less than 5 hours per week in biblical training and eighty-plus hours per week of non-biblical training through the influence of friends, TV, computers, games, and school.

The author shared another statistic that would forever change our thinking on how to raise children: 93% of homeschooled children continue to attend church as adults!

As we began thinking about this statistic, it made perfect sense. Where we spend our time is an indication of our priorities and shapes our relationships and our lives. If we want to influence our children to have the same beliefs and core values that we do, we needed to increase the amount of time they spend with us!

Homeschooling would allow Debbie to pour her heart and time into our children. Debbie prayed and prayed about this, and I gave her the complete freedom to choose whether we'd homeschool or send them to a Christian school.

She decided to homeschool our children, and we've continued to do so ever since. We are beginning to see the fruit of this decision. People regularly comment on how well-mannered our children are. Both children are very advanced academically, and both children love Jesus.

As I mentioned earlier, our home is less than 2 miles from where Debbie grew up and where her parents currently live. I had met my grandparents on my dad's side once and only saw my grandparents on my mom's side for Thanksgiving and Christmas.

Our children have an incredible relationship with their grandparents. They visit them regularly and stay with them during the times when Debbie and I get away for a weekend. They accepted Monica as their own granddaughter, and Amanda has a great relationship with them as well.

My mom lived about 4 hours away when Monica and Amanda were younger. Monica developed a strong relationship with her, and she took Amanda on as her own grandchild.

Mom got very sick and went to the hospital when Nathan was almost 2. This turned out to be a huge blessing, as we found an apartment for her that was only 2 miles from our house, and she moved in there.

When the kids were younger, Debbie would swing by

to pick Mom up and she'd spend 3 or 4 days a week with them at our home, just hanging out and playing. Mom is on oxygen now. It's more difficult for her to come to our house, so we still try to visit her at least once a week.

As I mentioned earlier, my dad lives about 5 hours away and we visit him every summer. Watching him with the kids is incredible. God is blessing him through what he missed when we were kids. Dad comes over and visits us a couple of times a year for a week at a time. He has an incredible relationship with our kids.

"Honor your father and mother"—which is the first commandment with a promise—"so that it may go well with you and that you may enjoy long life on the earth."
—Ephesians 6:2-3

Debbie and I are thankful that we decided very early in our marriage to honor our parents, and we are now experiencing the promise of this scripture, enjoying our life on earth. Our hope and prayer is that when our children grow up, they will instinctively choose to live close to us so that their children will have a strong relationship with us, just as they did with their grandparents.

One of our goals for our children is that they would each have the heart of a servant, and a constant desire to serve and help others. Years ago we started "Serving Sundays" and served our neighbors by picking up garbage and helping them out in their yards with our kids. We have lost this habit but I hope to pick it up again soon. Debbie models servanthood better than anybody I know and is passing this to our children. We are teaching them 4 magic words that we believe will transform their lives and reflect their hearts:

How Can I Help?

When their mom comes home from the grocery store, I ask the kids to meet her in the garage and ask, "How can I help?" Every time they ask, I see Debbie begin to glow. I'm also teaching these magic words to the boys on my football team. Their parents regularly ask me, "What have you done to my son? It's awesome—he's always asking to help!"

I encourage you to begin teaching your children these 4 magic words. I believe they will change their lives.

Debbie and I have prioritized our relationship because we believe the strength of our family can never be greater than the strength of our relationship with each other and with Christ. The stronger we are, the stronger our family will be. I've already talked about some of the rituals we've put in place including a date night at least once per month and 2 to 3 getaways per year. I believe both of these rituals reawaken our romantic love for each other and are foundational to the strength of our relationship.

Study after study has proven the truth of the old adage, "Couples that pray together, stay together." According to a recent Gallup poll, "Among married couples who attend church together regularly, the divorce rate is 1 out of 2. That is the same statistic for marriages outside the church. However, among married couples who pray together daily, the divorce rate drops to 1 out of 1,153." Debbie and I haven't built the habit of praying together daily, but we do pray together multiple times per week, and believe it is another reason that our marriage is so strong.

There are many tactical details associated with being married. Years ago, Debbie and I began the habit of conducting "Business Meetings" to discuss these details. We meet together weekly and discuss these details, including the following agenda:

- Open in prayer

- What are the highlights and lowlights of the previous week?
- How is our relationship doing?
- What are our dreams and goals for the future?
- What is on our calendar for the next 6 months? Are we prioritizing our time with what is most important to us?
- How are our finances?
- How are each of us doing with exercise and self-care?
- How are each of our children doing?
- How effectively are we honoring our parents?
- How are we strengthening our friendships?
- What is our detailed calendar for the upcoming weeks?
- Close in prayer

Our business meetings have dramatically affected our marriage. In the past, our marriage and lives have been so strong that we've discontinued our business meetings. Within only a few months, though, we discovered that we weren't as connected to each other and our relationship was deteriorating.

We remind ourselves of the importance of our meetings and re-establish our habit of meeting together. Our first meeting is always rocky; we have pent up frustrations, and they come out during the meeting. Within a few weeks, however, we hit a rhythm and are able to finish a meeting within an hour. We've recently decided to have our business meetings at 6:00 in the morning on Mondays, prioritizing our family business above all other business in the week.

On February 28, 1999, I penned the dream that I never thought would come to pass:

My Dream

My dream is to have a Christian family. We live in a small town with clean streets and sidewalks. The sun is out, and I'm playing catch with my children in the yard. The 100-year-old shade tree shades our home. My wife calls us in for dinner, and we pray together at the table. We enjoy our dinner and talk about our day. Everyone is smiling, and you can feel the love in the air. After dinner, I do the dishes with the children. We go into the living room and play games until bedtime. I put the children to bed, and my wife and I pray with them. When we wake up, breakfast is on the table and we all start our day together. I go to work, and get home right after the kids do, and we start again. Peace, Love, Joy—these embody my dream.

Last night my wife and I prayed with our children before they went to bed. We do this every night. This morning as I was writing this book I stopped for a while to have breakfast with them. Later this afternoon I'll play catch with Nathan in our yard: the same yard that has a 100-year-old Maple tree shading it. My wife will have dinner on the table and we'll talk about our day, laughing and smiling and enjoying the peace of our Christian home that is filled with love. The dream took much longer to happen than I would have hoped, but I kept working toward the dream and I waited. Today and every day I live the dream that I never thought would be possible on that day.

God knew what I didn't know: I'd have to experience incredible amounts of pain for a number of years before He could bless me with the fulfillment of this dream. My decision to accept the pain and grow from it has changed me, and I believe it will end the generational curses in my bloodline that have plagued my family.

How about you? Will you choose to accept your pain so that God can transform you into the person He has created you to be? My wish and sincere prayer in writing this book is that I might inspire you with the hope and courage you need to find joy in your pain and grow from it.

My dream for the second half of my life is to add value to your life, helping you change through your pain so that you too can live the dream that He's placed in your heart!

I would love to talk with you and hear your story. Please send an email to ***damon@paindriveschange.com*** with the subject line "I finished your book!" and I'll schedule a phone call with you.

Thank you for allowing me to share my story with you. Please let me know how I can help!

Damon Stoddard
www.paindriveschange.com

All praise goes to God, Father of our Lord Jesus, the Anointed One. He is the Father of compassion, the God of all comfort. He consoles us as we endure the pain and hardship of life so that we may draw from His comfort and share it with others in their own struggles.
—2 Corinthians 1:3-4

13
Epilogue

Two days after I started writing this book I went for my morning run. Like most mornings, I put on my headphones and listened to worship music. On this morning I was listening to Jeremy Camp when his song "There Will Be a Day" began to play. My mom's health had been declining and she had just come home from rehab after surgery to remove cancer from a portion of her colon. Mom was on oxygen and suffered from extreme anxiety and fear of death. Tears flowed from my eyes as I listened to the chorus:

But I hold on to this hope and the promise that He brings
That there will be a place with no more suffering

There will be a day with no more tears,
no more pain,
and no more fears

There will be a day when the burdens of this place,
Will be no more,
we'll see Jesus face to face

I felt God speaking to me through these words and my tears. I didn't know how long mom would live, and I needed to honor my mom through my writing. I needed to ask her to write a letter for my book. I knew her letter would offer hope to all of the moms that would read my book. I ran for a few more minutes and decided I'd call her and ask.

"Mom, would you write a letter for my book?" I asked.

"Son, grandma always thought I'd be an author but I never was. I'd love to write a letter. My hands are shaky and I can barely write so you'll have to help me" she responded.

"Thank you, I'll stop by in the next few days and we can talk about it." I said.

I was overwhelmed with joy. As I ran in the morning sun I raised my hands to the heavens worshipping God with tears in my eyes. This was His will.

A few days later I pulled a chair close to mom so we could hear each other and I asked her to share her story. I furiously typed my notes; I didn't want to miss anything. I watched the tears flow from my mom's eyes as she shared about giving up her children. I held her hand and told her it was ok as we cried together.

Over the next few months I stopped by her house and read my book to her as she sat in her chair. "I'm proud of you, son. This is going to be a bestseller," she said with pride.

One day I stopped by and she told me she'd written the letter. Her hands were very shaky, but she'd managed to write it out. I asked her to read it to me.

Her tears revealed the depth of her pain.

"A mother's nightmare....getting dark and no place to go....please help me....when I heard foster care my heart fell out....I need you to keep them together....."

My eyes welled up with tears as I gently held her hand.

"My children will be safe....my heart is broken. I have no choice.....the children have to go to different homes.....a mother's heart is breaking...."

"This was one of the hardest times of my life leaving my children. Tears are flowing as I have memories of that day in Wenatchee," she said as she finished.

I went to her chair and hugged her, telling her it was ok. "I am the man I am today because of that hard choice," I told her.

Mom shared many of the poor choices she had made in her life. She wasn't proud of the choices but she wanted to be honest. She had nothing to hide, and she knew that her honesty might help somebody in a similar situation.

I looked Mom in the eye and I told her "Mom, your sins are forgiven. As far as the east is from the west your sins are forgiven."

She admitted it was hard to accept forgiveness. I asked her if she'd asked for forgiveness from those she'd hurt the most including my oldest sister and my dad.

She said she hadn't asked for their forgiveness. I encouraged her to seek their forgiveness. A few weeks later she read a letter she'd written to my older sister asking for her forgiveness. She was exuberant with joy as she shared the text message she'd received from her daughter after sending the letter. "I forgave you a long time ago, Mom. "

Mom told me she was planning on writing a letter to my dad asking for his forgiveness, but her hands were too shaky to do so.

Mom went to the hospital a few days before Christmas with chest pain. I was at her bedside multiple times. She was in pain and experiencing fear and anxiety. She asked me if my book was a bestseller yet and I reminded her I hadn't published it, but if it was God's will it would become a bestseller.

She told me she was in pain and asked me to pray for her. I held her hand and prayed that Jesus would take her pain away and remove her anxiety. As I walked out of her hospital room she said, "I love you, son, I'm proud of you."

These were her last words to me. I received a call from the hospital the next morning. Mom's heart slowed down and she died peacefully with the doctor and nurses by her side.

The day after her death I awoke early and went to the hospital to talk with the nurses that were by her side when she passed. Their names were Faith and Grace! They shared how they held her hand and comforted her, reminding her it was ok to go be with Jesus.

I am eternally grateful for the time I got to spend with mom during the writing of this book. My heart softened and I became closer to her than I've ever been.

Mom's dying wish was that all of her children would be together and love each other. She didn't have much money, but she saved all year and every Christmas we all went to her house for a Prime Rib feast. Mom left us some money and bought us Christmas dinner one last time. My 2 older sisters prepared the feast in her house a few days after her death. All of her children and most of her grandchildren and great grandchildren gathered together to honor her.

But mom left us all another gift. We discovered a box of her daily journals, a habit she'd started more than twenty years earlier. After the Prime Rib feast her whole family gathered in a circle and we read her Christmas journals. Every journal started with "Dear Jesus, Thank you for ....." and was filled with her words of gratitude for everything she had and for the blessing of her family. She ended every journal with "Guide me today, and protect my family." Tears filled the room as our whole family got to see mom's soul through her writing.

In her honor, we plan on continuing the Christmas tradition of a Prime Rib feast followed by the reading of her journals for years to come.

As I mentioned above, Mom's dying wish was that her children would love each other and be together. Prior to her death we chatted occassionally but rarely saw each other. Since Mom's death, we regularly text each other and are closer to one another than we've ever been. Her death is teaching us how to be a family, the family all of us longed for as children but didn't have.

We are sad that she's gone but we rejoice that she's in heaven with no more suffering, no more pain, and no more tears.

Mom's headstone will reflect her daily prayer that she wrote in her journals:

Dear Jesus,

Thank you for my family. Guide them and protect them until we meet again.

I love you, and I am proud of you, mom.

Your son,

—*Damon*

Thank you Jesus for my mom.

Notes

Introduction

1. James 1:2-4 NASB

Chapter 1

1. Mark 2:3-5 NIV
2. Men's Secret Wars by Patrick A. Means (Revel, 1999)
3. James 5:15 NASB

Chapter 2

1. Proverbs 29:18 KJV
2. Psalm 40:1-3 NIV
3. Proverbs 15:22 NASB

Chapter 3

1. Habakkuk 2:2 NASB
2. Hebrews 12:11 NASB
3. Habakkuk 2:2-4 NASB
4. 2 Timothy 1:7 KJV
5. Philippians 4:8 NASB
6. Proverbs 29:18 KJV
7. Ephesians 5:25 NIV

Chapter 4

1. Romans 12:2 ISV
2. Proverbs 18:20-21 NASB

Chapter 5

1. Matthew 3:17 NIV
2. www.fathers.com/statistics-and-research
3. Exodus 20:5 NLT

Chapter 6

1. 1 John 3:18 NIV
2. Hebrews 12:11-13 NASB

Chapter 7

1. Malachi 2:16 NLV
2. Ephesians 4:29 NASB
3. Proverbs 15:22 NIV
4. Love Must Be Tough: New Hope for Marriages in Crisis by James C. Dobson (Tyndale Momentum, 2007)

Chapter 8

1. 2 Corinthians 5:18-19 NIV
2. Reconcilable Differences by Jim A. Talley (Thomas Nelson, 2008)
3. Dating With Integrity by John Holzmann (Sonlight Curriculum, ltd, 2003)
4. Saving Your Second Marriage Before It Starts by Les & Leslie Parrott (Zondervan, 2001)
5. Love Must Be Tough: New Hope for Marriages in Crisis by James C. Dobson (Tyndale Momentum, 2007)
6. The 21 Irrefutable Laws of Leadership: Follow Them and People Will Follow You by John C. Maxwell (Thomas Nelson, 2007)
7. Reconciliation Instruction by Dr. Jim Talley (R&R Publishing, Inc., 2013)
8. John 15:1-2 NIV
9. Secrets of the Vine: Breaking Through to Abundance by Bruce Wilkinson and David Kopp (Multnomah Books, 2006)

Chapter 9

1. Exodus 20:5 NLT
2. Facing Love Addiction: Giving Yourself the Power to Change the Way You Love by Pia Melody, Andrea Wells Miller, & J. Keith Miller (HarperOne, 2003)
3. Ephesians 6:2-3 NIV
4. Love Is a Choice: The Definitive Book on Letting Go of Unhealthy Relationships by Robert Hemfelt, Frank Minirth, Paul Meier (Thomas Nelson, 2003)
5. Reconciliation Instruction by Dr. Jim Talley (R&R

Publishing, Inc., 2013)

Chapter 10

1. 1 Thessalonians 4:3-4 BSB
2. Too Close, Too Soon: Avoiding the Heartache of Premature Intimacy by Jim A. Talley & Bobbie Reed (Thomas Nelson, 2002)
3. Matthew 5:37 BSB
4. 1 John 1:19 BSB

Chapter 11

1. Revelation 21:5 NIV
2. Strong Fathers, Strong Daughters by Meg Meeker (Ballantine Books, 2007)
3. 1 Peter 5:8 NIV
4. "40" as written by Dave Evans, Adam Clayton, Lyrics © Universal Music Publishing Group.
5. "Praise You in This Storm" as written by Bernie Herms, John Mark Hall Lyrics © Sony/ATV Music Publishing LLC, Warner/Chappell Music, Inc.

Chapter 12

1. Deuteronomy 11:26-28 NIV
2. Psalm 127:3 NLT
3. An Elephant in the Living Room: A Leader's Guide for Helping Children of Alcoholics by Marion H. Typpo, Ph.D. & Jill M. Hastings, P.h.D. (Hazelden, 1994)
4. Disciple Like Jesus for Parents by Alan Melton & Paul Dean (Calvary Press, 2010)
5. Ephesians 6:2-3 NIV
6. Prayer-Saturaded Church by Cheryl Sacks (Nav-Press, 2007)
7. 2 Corinthians 1:3-4 VOICE

Chapter 13

1. "There Will Be a Day" as written by Christopher Andrew Carrabba, Lyrics © Universal Music Publishing Group

Damon Stoddard wrote his first book, *Pain Drives Change*, in 45 days. He built a thriving small groups ministry at his former church and led men's ministry while working full-time at Microsoft. Damon won numerous awards for his work in hardware quality including Xbox and Surface. He currently serves on the board of directors for one of the largest Christian junior football programs in Washington state. He and his wife Debbie live near Seattle and have 4 children. You can find more information at:

www.paindriveschange.com

Made in the USA
San Bernardino, CA
14 February 2020

64342881R00140